SAYS WHO?

SERVING GOD WITH CONFIDENCE

J. BRIAN FARISH

Copyright 2024

Copyright © 2024 by J. Brian Farish

All rights reserved. No part of this publication may be reproduced, distributed, or transmitted in any form or by any means, including photocopying, recording, or other electronic or mechanical methods, without the prior written permission of the author, except in the case of brief quotations embodied in critical reviews and certain other noncommercial uses permitted by copyright law.

Unless otherwise indicated, all Scripture quotations are from the ESV® Bible (The Holy Bible, English Standard Version®), © 2001 by Crossway, a publishing ministry of Good News Publishers. Used by permission. All rights reserved.

TABLE OF CONTENTS

DEDICATION	9
ACKNOWLEDGMENTS	13
PREFACE	15
CHAPTER 1: MAIN THEMES	23
Whose opinion really matters?	23
Commit and act	25
If you are still alive, it is not too late	27
Confidence in the end	29
CHAPTER 2: AUDIENCE	31
You believe God exists.	31
You believe the Bible is God's word to us.	32
You will be both seeker and a guide	33
CHAPTER 3: THE GREATEST COMMANDMENT	35
Love God = Keep His commandments	39

CHAPTER 4: WHO DO YOU WORSHIP?   45
    Omnipotent [All-powerful]   47
    Omniscient [All-knowing]   47
    Omnipresent [Always present]   48

CHAPTER 5: A CHANGING GOD?   51
    God's will doesn't change   51
    Does God really care about the details?   52
    The indulgent God vs the God of the Bible   53

CHAPTER 6: HOW DO YOU KNOW WHO YOU WORSHIP? 55

CHAPTER 7: DO YOU WORSHIP THE GOD OF THE BIBLE? 59
    New Testament Christianity isn't "mystical"   59
    God Almighty – Creator of the universe   61

CHAPTER 8: BASED ON WHAT?   65
    You can figure it out for yourself   66
    "Ask, seek, knock" promise.   66
    Christianity in hostile times   67

CHAPTER 9: HOW DO YOU HANDLE SCRIPTURE?   71
    The Bible is sufficient.   71
    The dangers of human logic   74
    "…give thought to do what is honorable in the sight of all."
    – Romans 12:17   76
    Salvation in the "Wait… what?" moments   77

CHAPTER 10: WHOSE OPINION MATTERS MORE?   79
    "So, isn't believing in God and living a 'good life' enough?"   79

CHAPTER 11: ATTITUDE CHECK   83
- Husbands and wives   83
- Homosexuality   84
- Transsexuality   86
- Women in leadership positions in the church   87
- Subjection to governmental authority   87
- Infinite forgiveness   88
- Marriage & divorce   89

CHAPTER 12: THE BELIEVER'S FOUNDATION   91
- The Bible is the only way we know God's will.   94
- The Old Testament is not a binding covenant on Christians.   95
- The New Testament is the complete description of God's will   97
- God doesn't change;
- Therefore, God's will for us doesn't change   98
- There will be consequences for unrepentant rebellion   98
- Satan wants you ignorant   99
- Truth   101
- Biblical authority spectrum   103

CHAPTER 13: PEACE AND CONFIDENCE IN THE END   105
- Callused knees are a good start   105
- "Whittlin' on God's end of the stick"   108
- "Seek ye first the Kingdom…"   109

CHAPTER 14: ASK, SEEK, KNOCK   111

APPENDIX 1: THE PRODIGAL'S PATH   113
- You can come back   114

APPENDIX 2: THE LATE WORKER'S HOPE	121
Don't delay	124
No one deserves salvation	125
How do I join the church?	125
How do I come to God?	130
With whom do I worship?	135

DEDICATION

This book is dedicated to my father and mother, **Robert Hilman Farish** and **Virginia Scott Farish**. As a child, in addition to relatively "normal kid" thinking, I would sometimes lie in bed at night and wonder why I had been blessed to be born into a family of faith. It probably sounds strange to some folks that a child would wonder about such things, but no one ever claimed I was a completely normal child. The randomness and (from a child's earthly point of view) unfairness of it bothered me. I didn't realize until I was much older that an additional point to ponder was why I had been blessed to be born to two loving parents willing to sacrifice so much for me.

While I still have not gotten a complete answer to the question, I have come to understand more about the nature of God's dominion and have accepted my obligation to bow to His will and try to redeem the time and blessings I have been given.

In any case, my parents did everything in their power to prepare me to be a Christian, and I know that many of my decisions caused them anxiety, heartache, and worry. But the seeds that they planted in my formative years while being choked out for a time eventually bore fruit, and I am eternally grateful for their love, guidance, and patience.

The lives they led and the examples they set were a large part of the guidance they provided. My father and I butted heads as only a father and son of Scottish ancestry can. I never really understood the depth of his love for me until he was gone, and even more surprisingly, I never understood the depth of my love for him until it was too late to demonstrate it. I can't wait to see him again and tell him so.

It was the example of love in action that my father provided that had the most significant effect on me. As I mentioned, we could butt heads mightily over some of my bad choices, but if I ever came to him broken by something I had done and in pain, there was no accusation, no "I told you so," only help in setting a better course and forgiveness. That example of a father's love and forgiveness has been essential to my understanding of God's love for us, and I am eternally grateful for it.

My mother was indeed a remarkable example of a Christian wife. I never saw my mother and father fight. **Never.** That fact has become increasingly amazing to me with every passing year because my mother was no simple-minded dishrag with no opinions. My parents had keen intellects and a voracious appetite for learning and supported and enabled each other in their spiritual and intellectual growth. But any differences of opinion were dealt with quietly and out of sight of curious little eyes. They dealt with difficult times throughout their marriage with grace and faith.

As with my father, my understanding and appreciation of the strength, faith, and love that my mother brought to their relationship, our family, and finally me has grown with each year since her passing. I look forward to our reunion someday.

Finally, I am indebted to my North Star and the love of my life, my wife, Linda. She has been a comfort in the hard times and a true joy in the good times.

When we are young and dreaming of our life partners, "worthy adversary" probably isn't one of the traits we list. But in retrospect, she has been the "iron sharpening iron" that I needed.

I am blessed beyond description and far beyond what I deserve.

ACKNOWLEDGMENTS

I am grateful to David Ladyman and Mark Casey for investing their time in reading an early draft and providing feedback and enhancements.

David's keen intellect and extensive writing and editor experience were comforting assets and terrifying realities. I cannot overstate his contribution to the book's technical details and the insights he gently offered where appropriate. David is one of a handful of people to whom I can take a spiritual matter with the confidence that a productive discussion can be had.

Many years of discussions with Mark have challenged me and provided perspectives that I might not have discovered on my own. The history has been long and colorful, from long discussions on snowy drives to ski areas in northern New Mexico and southern Colorado to tennis courts in Austin, TX.

If you have never tried to write a book and then get feedback on it before publishing it, you may not know just how precious that gift of time is. I do know and am grateful.

PREFACE

"The mass of men lead lives of quiet desperation."
– Henry David Thoreau

This book is for anyone living a life of quiet desperation and fear about their eternal destiny. Based on what I read in the Bible, I believe it is possible to face eternity with confidence.

When I started this book, many of my claims about facing the end confidently were based on others' observations and without personal experience. Since then, God has provided me with some insight and perspective that I'd like to share.

On September 7th, 2003, I had surgery for colon cancer. I was blessed with early detection and treatment. However, there was a period during the early diagnosis where the future was unclear.

Fast forward almost exactly 20 years, and on November 13, 2023, I had surgery to treat an aneurysm in my brain that had presented and was causing me some problems. As of this writing, I am blessed, and the treatment seems effective.

My intent is not to "overshare" personal details or make you uncomfortable. Still, the difference in my perspective to what I thought might be my last moments on earth in these two episodes 20 years apart was uplifting for me, and I hope it will inspire you.

In the first episode, I was hurt and scared, and I remember lying in my hospital bed looking out a window over a gravel rooftop, wondering if that was the last view I'd ever have.

As I prayed for mercy, I knew that I wasn't "ready"; the cares of this life had distracted me, and while I struggled to cling to my faith, my priorities just weren't where they needed to be. So, for the most part, my prayers centered on asking for forgiveness and more time.

God was merciful and gave me more time.

I want to say that I was instantly transformed upon departing the hospital and focused on the right priorities from that day forward, but some of us are just slow learners, and the process was much more gradual than it probably should have been.

However, in the 20 years that passed, I shifted some priorities and focused on reading what the Bible spells out for me as God's plan and focusing on what the Word told me of His expectations.

One of the best things I did was implement a daily 30-minute session with my Bible being read to me by my phone. Some days, I was more focused than others, but the word was always there, and I could expose myself to the entire New Testament in less than two months.

I discuss the beginnings of this book elsewhere so that I won't repeat it, but the whole process brought me to the second episode, where I was facing eternity. I realized that my prayers in the two instances were markedly different.

Whereas episode one prayers were for forgiveness, mercy, and more time, episode two prayers were for forgiveness, mercy, care for my loved ones and accepting me into eternal rest.

I had finally found the confidence I had seen in others, which had eluded me for so long.

That confidence wasn't born of some "better felt than told" emotional wish; it came from understanding the Almighty's promises about His expectations, love, understanding, and mercy.

That confidence was a rational belief based on the facts and promises presented in God's word.

You can have that confidence and peace if you focus on listening to Him and tune out some earthly opinions that clutter up the message.

Referring to the Thoreau quote, I believe that the quiet desperation that many feel may come from a variety of reasons:

1) They know they are too focused on this life and have not "laid up their treasures in heaven."

2) They have been misled about what God expects and have set expectations for themselves for sinless perfection that are impossible to achieve.

3) They have created a god in their own image who will tolerate or even encourage them to live lives that the God of the Bible prohibits. Because they don't want to admit this to themselves or their friends and family, they pretend this god is the God of the Bible, but deep in their hearts, they know that it is a lie, and it gnaws at them.

The Bible tells us about God, the Creator of the Universe. Such a magnificent, powerful being should be able to communicate His wishes to His creation. If I believe that, then the solution to having a peaceful heart is reading His communicated will and earnestly trying to follow it.

We'll discuss priorities in more detail, but spiritual salvation is fundamentally a "full-time" job. The legitimate cares of this life distract us, but we need to constantly refocus our efforts on what is essential.

You don't check in on it occasionally on holidays, weddings, funerals, or the odd weekend.

God Almighty, the Creator of the Universe, can communicate His wishes to His creation in a manner that can stand alone, without editing by his creation, for all time.

Again, while this seems simple, many miss the fact that if one wants to please God Almighty, it makes sense to read the instructions He left behind and follow them as closely as is humanly possible.

If you are inclined to try to slander that attitude as "legalism," then you probably won't find much value here. If you are curious and read on, I hope my application of the revealed truth becomes clear and persuasive.

The truths in this book [the quotations from scripture] are eternal and essential, and while their power and value cannot be diminished, my biggest fear is that my limitations as a writer might obscure some of them. I hope you believe me when I tell you that I have prayed repeatedly for wisdom, guidance, and for God to help me take myself out of this and share only "the truth."

I have relied heavily on scripture, the only legitimate foundation for a Christian life, and have tried to limit my interpretations and applications. Where I cannot resist "thinking out loud," I have tried to label that content as such clearly.

My goal is to inspire you to read the Bible for yourself with faith, hope, and prayer and to "work out your own salvation."

There is nothing in this book that is intentionally written to be harsh or damning from the perspective of the author. However, the fact is, in a society as corrupt and degenerate as ours has become, a simple quotation of God's truth is often a damning statement. So, if something is offensive to you, ask yourself a couple of questions before walking away from the book:

1) Is what is offensive to me a conclusion that the author has made? If so, compare the conclusion to any scriptures that support it, and always follow your sincere understanding of what the scripture tells you.

2) Is what is being taught by the scripture what is offensive to me? If so, you have an obvious choice to either bend your will to God's or not. It is as simple as that. Christians who follow God's will are going to be a peculiar people in a corrupt society. We will be very different and must be strong enough to accept that.

I hope that after you've read this book when someone asks you why you believe something ("Oh yeah! Says who?"), you will not point to this book, your parents, someone in a church, or some "Biblical scholar." I want you to be able to point to the Bible with confidence and peace of mind, which will only come from a dedicated study of the Bible on your part.

I also want to encourage that "Oh yeah! Says who?" spirit in you. You are responsible for pleasing God and finding salvation. Not a church, not a preacher/rabbi/priest, not a pastor, not an elder, not a deacon, not your parents, not your spouse... YOU. And when anyone begins to press ideas, beliefs, and expectations on you based on their opinion, tradition, habit, or expediency, I hope that after reading this, you will at the very least ask YOURSELF... "Says who?" And if the answer is not genuinely Biblical, I hope you follow what you read in the Bible.

"A soft answer turns away wrath, but a harsh word stirs up anger."
– Proverbs 15:1

An interesting observation shared by a friend was that when anger starts to be felt when discussing Biblical topics, it is motivated by fear of not having a ready scriptural answer for an opinion. Anger can indicate that we are trying to be "right" instead of trying to find "the truth." It is wise to bear that in mind, both for ourselves to help us manage our own actions and to evaluate the mental state of the person with whom we are having the discussion.

We should always frame our assertions as Biblically based and non-inflammatory as possible, always choosing Godly love as our guide. "Arguing about religion" is pointless and should be carefully avoided in favor of searching for the truth.

Godly love rarely "feels good." It involves exercising self-control and choosing words and actions intended to produce thoughtful consideration by the action's target rather than making them feel silly or embarrassed. So, most of the clever turns of phrase we see folks include in Biblical discussions are more motivated by pride and a need to "win" than a sincere desire to motivate someone to consider a different position or help someone find the truth.

I believe most "clever" phrasing is intended to impress the listener/reader with the intellect/insight of the speaker. We have to be careful to keep our pride in check and always remember that there is One opinion that matters in things eternal.

CHAPTER 1:
MAIN THEMES

Whose opinion really matters?

"Givens"

There are some fundamental truths that we'll be referring to, so I want to list them as a foundation:

Given #1	God is all-powerful (omnipotent)	Genesis 1:1
Given #2	God is all-knowing (omniscient)	1 John 3:20
Given #3	God is in control (sovereign)	Romans 9:14-21
Given #4	God cannot lie	Hebrews 6:18
Given #5	God is eternal	Romans 1:23
Given #6	Humans are none of these things.	Romans 9:20-21

After reading this list of givens, a logical conclusion should be obvious. The Creator of the Universe isn't looking to us for what is acceptable, and the arrogance it takes to think that He does is truly amazing. The only way to get to that level of error is to abandon any respect for

God's will and His word and to presume that humanity occupies a much loftier position in the hierarchy of the universe than is accurate.

If we genuinely believe in a God who can speak entire universes into existence... all the galaxies, stars, planets, black holes, and comets... not to mention all the mountains, forests, animals, birds, sea creatures... and man, how silly it is to presume that a God of that magnificence is going to ask His creation to adjudicate the cosmic constraints of right and wrong or good and evil.

And if you don't believe in that God, the God described in the Bible, don't pretend to be worshipping that God. Please acknowledge that you are worshipping something you created from your imagination because you cannot have it both ways.

> *"Everything that I command you, you shall be careful to do. You shall not add to it or take from it."*
> *– Deuteronomy 12:32*

The title of this book has changed as I've worked out how to present the message. However, I realized that the core issue that must be resolved before digging deeper into God's will for us is to make sure that we are considering the proper sources of guidance for understanding that will.

The parable of the wise and foolish builder in Matthew 7:24-27 illustrates the importance of building our beliefs on a solid foundation (God's word) versus a weak foundation (man's opinions).

Commit and act

It is also important to note the "do" in this passage. It doesn't say, "heareth these words, smiles angelically, and ignores them."

> *"Everyone then who hears these words of **mine and does them** will be like a wise man who built his house on the rock. **25** And the rain fell, and the floods came, and the winds blew and beat on that house, but it did not fall, because it had been founded on the rock. **26** And everyone who hears these words of **mine and does not do them** will be like a foolish man who built his house on the sand. **27** And the rain fell, and the floods came, and the winds blew and beat against that house, and it fell, and great was the fall of it."*
> *– Matthew 7:24-27 (emphasis mine)*

You can figure it out for yourself

I believe in the omnipotent God who created the heavens and the earth in the beginning.

> *"In the beginning, God created the heavens and the earth."*
> *– Genesis 1:1*

So much of what is contained in this book hinges on those ten words, and the significance of those words should inform your approach to the Bible.

If they are untrue, you should stop reading for anything but literary value, beginning with Genesis 1:2.

If they are authentic, it makes sense that a God who is powerful enough to create the heavens and the earth could ensure that His will was communicated to his creation and kept available, intact, to that creation through the millennia.

If they are authentic, it is <u>not</u> "legalism" to turn to the Bible to learn what God's will is for us; it makes good sense. Whenever you hear someone complaining about "legalism," you need to be on the lookout for exactly where they start adlibbing their opinions into God's will.

The problem is that humanity is lazy. Rather than going to the Bible and reading and doing, they let someone else interpret scripture for them and then tell them what to do. This book aims to help you understand why that is a bad idea and how each of us is responsible for " working out our own salvation."

The most important subject you will ever consider is how you learn God's will for you and how you handle that knowledge. Your choices will decide where you spend eternity. Your understanding of God's will is not something to entrust to the most glib or confident speaker. It is not something to ignore and hope it will go away. You MUST engage and take an active role in your eternal well-being.

> "Therefore, my beloved, as you have always obeyed, so now, not only as in my presence but much more in my absence, **work out your own salvation** with fear and trembling."
> – Philippians 2:12 (emphasis mine)

The Bible is very clear that each of us is responsible for **<u>our own</u>** salvation, and God has promised in His word that we can figure it out and that if we turn to Him and diligently seek Him, we can find Him.

One of the paradoxes of writing this book is that the most important message is to go to the Bible to find out what God wants from you and stop relying on earthly influences, human books (like THIS book), preachers, church doctrine, etc.... because, as we will see, God has PROMISED that His word is sufficient and that you can do it.

However, "...work out your own salvation..." is not the same as "go out and start making things up for yourself." There are apparent truths and requirements in the New Testament about who God wants us to be, what God wants us to do, and how God wants us to serve Him. Just because societal norms have moved away from Biblical principles does not mean God's will has changed. Part of your "work out your own salvation" will be deciding whose opinion matters more... yours, your family's, society's, or God's.

You don't need a "blessing" from any human being or earthly organization.

We will see that there is one church of significance to your salvation, and only One determines that church's membership. Our language has confused us about exactly what "the church" is. God and only God determines the church's membership, and He doesn't ask any mortal beings for their "okay." We'll discuss that at length later.

If you are still alive, it is not too late

If you are blessed to live long enough, there comes a point where the inevitability of your mortality becomes "real" to you. You may become personally conscious of it because of the loss of a friend or a loved one or some significant personal experience (illness or some other challenge). It is at these times that Satan likes to "get in your ear" and tell you that it is too late, God couldn't possibly forgive you for waiting so long, etc. Satan uses our lack of understanding of the nature of God and His love for us to cultivate doubt and, in many cases, to cause us to give up.

Your salvation is a matter between you and God. It doesn't matter what your parents think. It doesn't matter what your wife or kids think. It doesn't matter what any priest, rabbi, preacher, pastor, elder, deacon, synod, conference, convention, or temple says. The ONLY thing that matters is your willingness to read the Bible and submit to God's will as found there. NONE of those parties just mentioned will be sitting in judgment of your life on the final day.

If you are taking the time to read this, it is a fair assumption that you have some level of either anxiety or curiosity. You either once felt like you had faith and were doing the right thing and have strayed from that, or you have never really been that focused on serving God and, while curious, feel like it would be hypocritical to turn to God late in life.

The central theme of this book is that if you once believed, you are never too far away from God to return to Him, and if you have never considered yourself a believer, if you have breath in you to believe, repent, and obey, it's never too late. Satan is real, and he knows how to mess with your head and whisper just precisely the right words to instill fear, doubt, and discouragement. Don't listen to him; listen to what God has said to you in His word. Believe the promises He has made, and you will find the peace available to His flock.

Over the years, the focus of many organized religions has shifted to many priorities besides communicating the pure gospel to souls who need it. The central theme of this book, finding your way to God, is that you don't need ANY book other than the Bible. If you reach a point where you decide to either give this book away or throw it away because you've realized that the Bible is the only thing you need, I've accomplished my goal.

Confidence in the end

Confidence and peace of mind found nowhere else come from a complete knowledge of God's promises about our salvation, a sincere desire to please Him, and a commitment to humble ourselves to Him above all else.

We all stumble, and the minute we do, Satan is right there, whispering, "Give up... You know you aren't worthy..." Well, the fact is, none of us is "worthy," but all of us have been offered grace if we will lay claim to it. The trick is to keep getting up every time we stumble and try again. God is not up above us sitting on His throne waiting to damn us, he is rooting for us to succeed, and we just need to keep looking to Him. He has set out precise expectations, and He WILL hold us accountable for bending our knees to His will. However, his awareness of our frailties led him to provide us with a path to redemption, and we would be foolish if we failed to make use of it.

As we work on becoming more loving and forgiving, we begin to understand the nature of God's love and how it might be possible for Him to forgive us and welcome us in. There is peace in that, and I wish that for all of you.

CHAPTER 2:
AUDIENCE

This work was initially conceived as an encouragement for wayward and backsliding Christians. Still, as I worked through it, I realized that many of the topics that had to be discussed would be of value to new Christians and those who may have become curious about Christianity later in life. As with any subject of any significance, many of the topics were related to other topics, and the scope grew.

To contain the scope of the effort and provide focus, some arbitrary boundaries must be set, and some assumptions about the audience must be made.

You believe God exists.
This book is not a book of apologetics; I'm not here to convince you there is a God. Many quality works make a robust case for at least a rational curiosity about whether there is a God, but that is not the

purpose of this work. The book, *"I Don't Have Enough Faith to be an Atheist,"* is an excellent place to start.

However, many think that they are worshipping the God of the Bible when, in reality, they worship a god who is of their own imagination or who has been created for them. It is impossible to successfully worship the God of the Bible while disregarding what He has explicitly given as instruction and guidance. We will examine this aspect of God's nature in more detail and provide the scriptural basis for this perspective.

You believe the Bible is God's word to us.
As we will examine later, the Bible asserts that it is the only source to know God's will. Therefore, either that is a true statement, or the Bible is a false document immediately disqualified as a source of God's will.

At its core, this is a book about purposeful Christianity.

Many of us were born into Christian families and drifted along doing what we were told while we lived under our parents' roof. However, as soon as we were freed from those guiding influences, some of us made some choices that we regret. As we regained a faith-based focus, many questions we may have had along the way returned, demanding resolution. I refer to this as the "Prodigal's path."

Others may not ever have been particularly spiritual but have reached a point in life where they are thinking about eternity, or possibly they have experienced a significant emotional event that has made them aware of their mortality. They are curious about spiritual matters but hesitate to commit to studying and changing their lives out of a feeling of unworthiness or possibly even hypocrisy. I refer to this as the "Late worker's hope."

As we'll discuss, Jesus addressed both scenarios in parables, and there is no legitimate reason for anyone still alive to hesitate to turn to God with complete confidence that salvation is possible.

We must find ways of overcoming the discouragement and fear that is Satan's most potent weapon against all who would try to follow God. Satan uses discouragement and fear to break down the resolve of wayward Christians who want to return to God. He uses fear to cause those who might turn to God later in life to hesitate, thinking it may be too late.

You will be both seeker and a guide

One of the fundamental themes of this study is personal responsibility. We each have a race to run and an individual search for the truth to conduct. But we also have a responsibility to help as many others find their way to God as possible. With that in mind, from time to time, the perspective of this discussion will shift from your personal search for the truth to helping others in their search and maintaining a loving attitude.

CHAPTER 3:
THE GREATEST COMMANDMENT

Many of the topics we must discuss will sound harsh to some, and the true nature of the God of the Bible will be a shock to many who have been taught the concept of a god who finds all their choices acceptable.

With that in mind, doing a quick "setting of context" for everything we will discuss as we go on this journey is helpful.

One of the biggest challenges some have in discussing matters of faith is the desire for **their belief** to be "right."

Please understand that this is an entirely different attitude than a desire to be right. The desire to prove one's belief right approaches all discussions in an adversarial manner, while the desire to BE right engages with a desire to learn and conform to God's truth.

We will examine man's belief vs. God's truth more deeply, but for now, the difference in attitude matters because the latter perspective (a desire to BE right) will drive a thoughtful, calm examination and discussion of scripture. The former attitude (a desire to have personal belief proven right) inspires argument, defensiveness, and accusation.

We must all monitor our hearts and tongues when examining spiritual matters. This is because everything else, without a desire to find the truth motivated by Godly love, wastes precious time. Love, as the central element of our spiritual pursuits, gives significance and value to our journey.

An honest examination of the scripture reveals that action is required for salvation. However, as we'll see in 1 Corinthians 13, an obsession with prioritizing activities over the right motivations is counterproductive.

But before the Apostle Paul shared that, Jesus established the priority of us loving our Creator and our fellow humans when questioned by the lawyer, documented in Matthew 22:35-40:

> *"And one of them, a lawyer, asked him a question to test him.*
> ***36** "Teacher, which is the great commandment in the Law?"*
> ***37** And he said to him, "You shall love the Lord your God with all your heart and with all your soul and with all your mind.*
> ***38** This is the great and first commandment. **39** And a second is like it: You shall love your neighbor as yourself. **40** On these two commandments depend all the Law and the Prophets."*
> *– Matthew 22:35-40*

When the lawyer approached Jesus with the question of the greatest commandment, it is important to note that Jesus didn't correct him or quibble; he told him, "Love the Lord thy God." But Jesus didn't stop there; He gave a "second like unto it," and that was to "love thy neighbor as thyself."

The Apostle Paul to the Corinthians emphasizes the relative importance of WHY we do what we do versus WHAT we do in 1 Corinthians 13. Our actions don't benefit us spiritually without the right "why" behind them.

> "If I speak in the tongues of men and of angels, but have not love, I am a noisy gong or a clanging cymbal. **2** And if I have prophetic powers, and understand all mysteries and all knowledge, and if I have all faith, so as to remove mountains, but have not love, I am nothing. **3** If I give away all I have, and if I deliver up my body to be burned, but have not love, I gain nothing."
> – 1 Corinthians 13:1-3

For a moment, consider what an example of Christianity a person would seem to be if they exhibited all the traits Paul enumerates. This person would be a profound public speaker, even able to speak in many languages. They would be brilliant and even able to foresee the future. Their faith would be so profound that he would be able to perform fantastic miracles. They would relinquish all their earthly wealth and donate it to feed the poor. Finally, in a supreme sacrifice, they give their body up to be burned. However, Paul says this person's efforts are fruitless from a spiritual profitability perspective if they are motivated by Godly love.

But Paul doesn't just throw the word "love" out there and leave it to be interpreted loosely... he describes the fruits of "love" so that we can recognize it in its true form.

> *"Love is patient and kind; love does not envy or boast; it is not arrogant 5 or rude. It does not insist on its own way; it is not irritable or resentful; 6 it does not rejoice at wrongdoing, but rejoices with the truth. 7 Love bears all things, believes all things, hopes all things, endures all things. 8 Love never ends. As for prophecies, they will pass away; as for tongues, they will cease; as for knowledge, it will pass away. 9 For we know in part and we prophesy in part, 10 but when the perfect comes, the partial will pass away. 11 When I was a child, I spoke like a child, I thought like a child, I reasoned like a child. When I became a man, I gave up childish ways. 12 For now we see in a mirror dimly, but then face to face. Now I know in part; then I shall know fully, even as I have been fully known. 13 So now faith, hope, and love abide, these three; but the greatest of these is love."*
> – *1 Corinthians 13:4-13*

I am reminded almost daily that loving my fellow humans is not the same as liking them. However, it is vitally important that any dislike is not allowed to grow into something that diminishes our fundamental desire for what is best for them.

> *"We love because he first loved us. 20 If anyone says, "I love God," and hates his brother, he is a liar; for he who does not love his brother whom he has seen cannot love God whom he has not seen. 21 And this commandment we have from him: whoever loves God must also love his brother"*
> – *1 John 4:19-21*

With Paul's teachings in 1 Corinthian 13, love becomes a critical foundational element to our salvation and spiritual acceptability to God. However, in modern religious organizations that want to emphasize obedience, it is mostly neglected in favor of indoctrination in guilt and inadequacy. In contrast, in religious organizations that want to take a permissive attitude about God's will, love is wholly misinterpreted to be a sort of "get out of jail free card," something soft, squishy, and more resembling what an indulgent grandfather or Santa Claus might offer.

Love God = Keep His commandments

"By this we know that we love the children of God, when we love God and obey his commandments. 3 For this is the love of God, that we keep his commandments. And his commandments are not burdensome."
– 1 John 5:2-3

There are two common extremes in approaching the Greatest and Second Greatest Commandments, and people tend to "favor" one perspective over the other.

At one extreme are the folks who see the word "love" and immediately assume that it is an emotional, warm, fuzzy thing loosely defined and exemplified by unconstrained tolerance for anything that the "loved" party wants to do.

At the other extreme are the folks who immediately jump to 1 John 5:2-3 and start creating a detailed list of all the commandments that have been explicitly given, implicitly given, or assumed to be implied by the actions of approved Biblical characters.

> *"Come to me, all who labor and are heavy laden, and I will give you rest. **29** Take my yoke upon you, and learn from me, for I am gentle and lowly in heart, and you will find rest for your souls. **30** For my yoke is easy, and my burden is light."*
> *– Matthew 11:28-30*

This invitation from Jesus cuts both ways... the "yoke is easy," and the "burden is light," but there is still a yoke and a burden, and it is up to us to accept that yoke and to take up that burden.

Please note that **what I'm about to say is my personal understanding**, and you need to develop your own understanding in working out your own salvation. That said, I believe that the truth lies somewhere in the middle of the two extremes mentioned. We will examine some examples of God's displeasure when His creation has presumed to disregard His instructions, so there is no rational argument for being careless in determining how God wants us to worship Him and what He wants us to do as Christians.

However, referring again to 1 Corinthians 13:1-3, we are cautioned against getting obsessed with the mechanics of worship or the external appearance of righteousness and neglecting the cultivation of a loving spirit as the foundation for our worship and service.

> *"If I speak in the tongues of men and of angels, **but have not love**, I am a noisy gong or a clanging cymbal. **2** And if I have prophetic powers, and understand all mysteries and all knowledge, and if I have all faith, so as to remove mountains, **but have not love**, I am nothing. **3** If I give*

> *away all I have, and if I deliver up my body to be burned,* **but have not love,** *I gain nothing."*
> – *1 Corinthians 13:1-3 (emphasis mine)*

It is very easy for people to become focused on actions because, compared to intent, actions are very easy to discern. This is at the heart of the lawyer's question to Jesus, "Which is the great commandment...?" i.e., On what do I need to focus?

Jesus didn't correct the lawyer but expanded the scope of the answer, indicating that there is indeed a "greatest commandment" and a very closely related "greatest commandment–part 2." Then, Jesus further asserts that these two commandments are the basis of the whole law and the prophets.

> *"And one of them, a lawyer, asked him a question to test him.* ***36*** *'Teacher, which is the great commandment in the Law?'* ***37*** *And he said to him, 'You shall love the Lord your God with all your heart and with all your soul and with all your mind.* ***38*** *This is the great and first commandment.* ***39 And a second is like it****: You shall love your neighbor as yourself.* ***40*** *On these two commandments depend all the Law and the Prophets'."*
> – *Matthew 22:35-40 (emphasis mine)*

So, the Apostle Paul in 1 Corinthians 13:1-3 contrasts the relative importance of any good work that could be imagined to having love as the underlying motive, and love wins as the priority every time.

And Jesus said the sum of the law and the prophets is: Love God; Love your neighbor.

Based on what we read in scripture about love and works, would you be more comfortable standing in judgment answering for actions taken in a "gray area" decision based on doctrinal precision... or actions based on love and informed by an awareness of the limits of what we can know about anyone else's heart?

The word typically translated as "love" in the New Testament is the Greek word "agape." While I make no claims to being a Greek scholar, it is essential to understand what the original word meant in our own words because our modern word "love" is so overloaded with varying and often conflicting meanings that using that word without definition leaves the door open to some potentially unfortunate conclusions.

At the time the New Testament was written, three other words in the Greek language referred to concepts that modern society thinks of as "love:" phileo (to be a friend to/ have affection for), storge (familial love), and eros (sensual attraction).

We must know what God expects of us when he demands "agape" for Himself and our neighbors. While learning to phileo our enemies might be possible, it is NOT required. However, it IS required that we agape our enemies, so we'd better develop a clear idea of what that looks like.

To think that God's agape for us renders Him incapable of meting out justice to the rebellious and willfully disobedient is genuinely a dangerous misunderstanding.

> "For God so loved the world, that he gave his only Son, that whoever believes in him should not perish but have eternal life."
> – John 3:16

While this is one of the most encouraging passages in the New Testament, unfortunately, some take John 3:16 as a spiritual "blank check" to presume God's justice and ignore God's instructions in the New Testament. They take the word "love" here and assign a weak, emotional interpretation that attempts to nullify God's power, His justice, and, indeed, the true nature of His agape for us. The New Testament makes it clear that true love (agape) for God involves more than a syrupy smile and a gaze heavenward.

> *"For this is the love of God, that we keep his commandments. And his commandments are not burdensome."*
> *– 1 John 5:3*

These passages don't leave any room for doubt about the question. Obedience is an essential part of loving God.

> *"Whoever has my commandments and keeps them, he it is who loves me. And he who loves me will be loved by my Father, and I will love him and manifest myself to him."*
> *– John 14:21*

But some still think that God will take whatever scraps of time they cannot fill with work, football games, TV, kid's functions, etc.... smile indulgently, and usher them into the Pearly Gates.

THAT god... the god who they are worshipping, is NOT the God described in the Bible.

You aren't going to "drift" into Heaven.

So, we all need to ask ourselves, knowing our hearts as only we and God can, "Am I really prioritizing God's will in my life?"

In addition to all the visible, tangible actions that people can see, are we really doing them for the right reasons? Are the actions truly motivated by agape? Agape is forgiving. Am I constantly working on forgiving those who have wronged me in the past? Am I trying to be more patient and forgiving day to day?

But many, upon finally accepting that there is a "do" component to salvation, run helter-skelter into a no less problematic obsession with commands and works.

God has been very clear that while obedience (works) is a part of His plan and, combined with the proper condition of heart, is essential in accessing grace, they are insufficient by themselves, and it is impossible for mortal man to live a life pure enough to earn salvation.

> *"If we say we have no sin, we deceive ourselves, and the truth is not in us.* **9** *If we confess our sins, he is faithful and just to forgive us our sins and to cleanse us from all unrighteousness.* **10** *If we say we have not sinned, we make him a liar, and his word is not in us."*
> *– 1 John 1:8-10*

So, once we have decided that we need to "do" things to serve the God of the Bible, how do we decide what to do?

Many folks are willing to tell us what to do, but ultimately, the responsibility is on each of us. To that end, we must know how to establish a solid foundation.

CHAPTER 4:
WHO DO YOU WORSHIP?

Who do you worship?

The question may sound silly to most people reading this book, but it does bear discussion.

If your first thought was, "I worship God!" you might have assumed that the "... of the Bible" was implied or assumed. If this was your reaction, please be patient, walk with me awhile, and discuss "the God of the Bible." I promise there is a point to this.

> *This is a quick aside about the role of the Old Testament. For many years, I focused on the New Testament because I believed (and still believe) that I am bound by the new covenant (testament), not the old.*

> *I am a little embarrassed to admit how many years it took me to realize that the Old Testament serves to introduce us to the God who we are worshipping under the New Covenant. Many of the truths revealed in the New Testament were framed for an audience of Jews who already knew the God of the Old Testament, His exacting standards when it came to His will, and how He reacted when His will was disregarded. While the specifics of God's expectations changed under the New Covenant, His attitude about obedience, reverence, and submission to His will did not.*

As noted earlier, the God of the Bible claims to have created everything.

> *"In the beginning, God created the heavens and the earth."*
> *– Genesis 1:1*

This opening verse of the Bible clearly sets the context for everything that is to follow.

We are God's creation; He sets the rules and expects us to follow them. A recurring theme in Deuteronomy is faithful obedience.

> *"You shall be careful therefore to do as the Lord your God has commanded you. You shall not turn aside to the right hand or to the left."*
> *– Deuteronomy 5:32*

When He communicated His will to the Israelites, He was unequivocal that they were not to add to or subtract from His instructions.

> *"You shall not add to the word that I command you, nor take from it, that you may keep the commandments of the Lord your God that I command you."*
> *– Deuteronomy 4:2*

...and as we noted earlier in ...

> *"Everything that I command you, you shall be careful to do. You shall not add to it or take from it."*
> *– Deuteronomy 12:32*

Omnipotent [All-powerful]

The "...created the heavens and the earth" statement does a pretty good job of establishing the capability to do anything He desires.

Jesus further clarified that He had all the authority to tell us what to do to achieve salvation.

> *"And Jesus came and said to them, "All authority in heaven and on earth has been given to me."*
> *– Matthew 28:18*

Omniscient [All-knowing]

The God of the Bible also clearly claims to know everything.

> *"...for whenever our heart condemns us, God is greater than our heart, and he knows everything."*
> *– 1 John 3:20*

> *"But even the hairs of your head are all numbered."*
> *– Matthew 10:30*

Omnipresent [Always present]

The combination of God's omnipotence (all-powerful) and omniscience (all-knowing) means that He knows everything we need and can do whatever is necessary to accomplish his will. This combination renders his physical presence moot.

However, God tells us that He will be there where two or three are gathered in His name. This seems to create a special holiness to that state of gathering rather than the structure in which it occurs (e.g., cathedral, church building, etc....).

> *"For where two or three are gathered in my name, there am I among them."*
> *– Matthew 18:20*

So, I promised you a "point" to all this discussion of creation and "omnis," etc....

With that in mind, I must ask the question...

Is the God who we just explored:

1) Incapable of communicating His wishes to his creation or ensuring that those wishes remain available?

2) A God who can be "outgrown" by His creation to the point that the creation needs to "correct" God's revealed will for man?

3) Likely to take lightly a flippant or disrespectful handling of His Truth? We didn't explore here the examples of the consequences of disobeying God's commandments, but the examples are many and devastatingly conclusive. We'll look at a couple of examples later on.

I worship the God of the Bible, and if the god whom you worship is incompetent, incapable, or tolerant of willful, unrepentant disobedience, then whoever that is... it is NOT the God of the Bible.

CHAPTER 5:
A CHANGING GOD?

I recently had a colleague recommend a book about spiritual matters. It was primarily benign and spoke to those with a broken and humbled spirit who felt beaten down by large denominational worship.

I could agree with most of the points except for the passionate attack on "legalism." The attack was made without defining or limiting the word's meaning, which means the term was left floating there as a handy life raft for anyone who felt overly constrained by God's words.

God's will doesn't change

A society that has abandoned a regular consumption of Biblical truths will fill that void with tradition, human desires, fads, and popular opinion. None of those things has any impact on God's will for humanity.

Feminism within the organization and worship in the church, sexual promiscuity, and deviancy may become widely accepted by a culture or society. Still, God's will on those subjects has been communicated **"once for all"** and is unchanging.

> "...contend for the faith that was once for all delivered to the saints."
> – Jude 1:3

So again, if the god you are worshipping changes or evolves to align himself with society, he may be many things, but he is NOT the God of the Bible. The God of the Bible was very clear in communicating His expectations.

Studying His revelation and submitting myself to His will makes me His servant, not a "legalist" per any derogatory definition.

Does God really care about the details?

Given God's clear revelation about how he wants to be worshipped and multiple examples of the results of not listening to God or ignoring His commands, the number of people willing to play "fast and loose" with worship is surprising.

Later, we will examine the examples of Nadab and Abihu's presumption of God's will, Uzzah's lack of attention to detail, and Ananias and Sapphira's blatant dishonesty and pride to demonstrate from scripture that God does not take disobedience to His instructions lightly and that he is willing to judge transgression.

The indulgent God vs the God of the Bible

I know many who cannot conceive of a God who would hold humanity accountable. They can hold this view because they do not bother to read God's will to know Him better.

The examples of Uzzah, Ananias and Sapphira, and Nadab and Abihu serve as cautionary tales. Still, there are so many additional examples of God's discipline in the Bible that there is no excuse for anyone who bothers to read the Bible to come away with an impression of a God who has no expectations of His creation.

However, an awareness of God's expectations of His creation in no way negates the magnificent gift of His grace, and we are foolish when we lose sight of that blessing. While God does set specific expectations and is clear in His communication of all the critical elements to our salvation, He is also aware of man's fallibility. He has freely made grace available to all who earnestly reach for Him but stumble.

The key is never to confuse a conscious choice to follow a path other than God's [willfulness] with an instance of stumbling on the path God has laid out [fallibility], for the former has consequences, and the latter has grace if we avail ourselves of it.

Examples would be:

- Knowingly harboring a grudge against someone who has done wrong to us in the past would be a willful act, whereas becoming aware of bitterness about it and trying to put it behind us would be more of an example of fallibility.

- Being caught up in a conversation that turns into gossip would be an example of fallibility, whereas enthusiastically pursuing and sharing gossip would indicate willfulness.

Figuring out the difference is simple. Regret and an intention to do better indicate fallibility, while complacency and apathy indicate willfulness.

Later, you'll get to do an "attitude check" and compare your desires and beliefs against what God has revealed to us in His word. Every time you feel the urge to argue with a passage, know that willfulness is probably the cause.

CHAPTER 6:
HOW DO YOU KNOW WHO YOU WORSHIP?

When asked the question, "Who do you worship?" the universe of answers can be sorted into those who reply:

1. "There is no God"
2. "I don't know if there is a God" (effectively the same as #1)
3. Someone other than God
4. God

As has been pointed out, the first and second responses are outside the scope of this effort, as is the case for anyone who chooses to worship someone or something other than the God of the Bible.

But among those who claim to worship the God of the Bible, there is a broad spectrum of beliefs ranging from, at one extreme, a God who just dropped us here, said "Be good," and then left us to determine right and wrong for ourselves to, at the other extreme, a God who put us here, gave us clear instructions about His expectations and expects us to follow what He has communicated to us.

It is a sad fact that the less people go to God's word, the more corrupt their impression of Him becomes over time. Combine Biblical ignorance with false teachers who are willing to tickle "itching ears" with lies, and you wind up with a society like ours.

And by "a society like ours," I mean a society of people who claim to be Christians who are offended at the very suggestion that God finds homosexuality, divorce (save for adultery), murder of unborn and newborn children, drunkenness, and on and on… sinful.

The ONLY way such nonsensical thinking can be fostered and tolerated is by either a complete ignorance of God's word or a blatantly rebellious attitude about God's will.

Too many people are spiritually lazy and want an excuse to indulge in the temptations the world offers.

God put all of us on this Earth with free will, so all the behaviors mentioned above and choices are available. However, what is NOT available to us is the knowing embrace, indulgence in, and tolerance of those behaviors AND an acceptable relationship with the God of the Bible.

Any god you choose to worship who finds those things acceptable is a god of your own creation and is NOT the "God of the Bible."

One way I heard of explaining this is that if you have a recipe for a chocolate cake and it calls for flour, eggs, butter, sugar, vanilla, milk, and cocoa and you opt to swap almond extract for the cocoa, you can still bake a cake, it just WON'T be a "chocolate cake." The same is true of the God who you choose to worship. If you change something that the Bible says the God of the Bible wants, you have created your own "god," but it is NOT the God of the Bible.

It is elementary. If you want to truly worship the God of the Bible, you MUST know what the Bible says that the God who it reveals expects of you. The only way to know that is to read the Bible for yourself and work to incorporate what you learn into your life.

To be clear, perfect execution of God's will is NOT required because there has only ever been One who could do that. As we discussed earlier, contrasting willfulness and fallibility, there is a vast difference between striving to obey and stumbling and willfully refusing to accept the parts of God's revelation that we find inconvenient. God knows our hearts, and He will judge us on the condition of our hearts that motivates our life choices.

God makes it clear in Exodus how He feels about "other" gods.

> *"You shall have no other gods before me."*
> *– Exodus 20:3*

…and in Ephesians, He makes it clear that He is the ONE way to salvation.

> *"There is one body and one Spirit—just as you were called to the one hope that belongs to your call— 5 one Lord, one faith, one baptism, 6 one God and Father of all, who is over all and through all and in all.."*
> *– Ephesians 4:4-6*

CHAPTER 7:
DO YOU WORSHIP THE GOD OF THE BIBLE?

New Testament Christianity isn't "mystical"

I've encountered some frightening levels of misunderstanding about Biblical Christianity among some folks claiming to be Christians. One lady went so far as to exclaim, "I invoke the Holy Spirit on you!" intending, I believe, that she was bestowing some special blessing on the person to whom she was writing.

I am very uneasy around people who throw around the name of the Holy Spirit because of the warning in Mark 3.

> "...but whoever blasphemes against the Holy Spirit never has forgiveness, but is guilty of an eternal sin..."
> – Mark 3:29

The lack of Bible study in our society has allowed some very unbiblical ideas to creep in. Unencumbered by Biblical constraints, they blossom because they are more entertaining than the day-to-day worship that God truly desires.

The problem is that many folks want Christianity to be something different than it is... an abiding commitment to humbling ourselves to God's will and simply striving to do what He instructs. There aren't any sparks, fireworks, or lightning, no ethereal music, or ghostly fogbanks, just a daily re-commitment to do God's will. It isn't that there is no joy; it just isn't the never-ending carnival ride that some people want it to be.

In almost every instance, the easy, fun, exciting, or gratifying option is the wrong one. A Godly life is about sacrifice and restraint, neither of which is trendy nor popular. Our me-me-me society doesn't value the quiet servant when there is a flashy alpha personality in the room. But God notices the soul of the servant and is pleased.

> *"But many who are first will be last, and the last first."*
> *– Matthew 19:30*

> *"Blessed are the poor in spirit, for theirs is the kingdom of heaven."*
> *– Matthew 5:3*

Many want smoke and wonders to be part of their worship of God, but Paul, in the first letter to the Corinthians, told them that once the Bible ("...the perfect...) was completed, there was no more need for signs and miracles ("...the partial...") and those would cease.

*"Love never ends. As for prophecies, they will pass away; as for tongues, they will cease; as for knowledge, it will pass away. **9** For we know in part, and we prophesy in part, **10** but when the perfect comes, the partial will pass away."*
– 1 Corinthians 13:8-10

God Almighty – Creator of the universe

God determines what is acceptable
As previously demonstrated, the Bible is very clear about God's expectations of His people regarding their role in society, their relationships in marriage, and their roles and methods of worship. However, society has deemed many of these expectations irrelevant and dismissible.

I submit that it is impossible to honestly believe in God, study His word, desire to serve Him, and hold such an attitude. If someone claims to believe in God and studies His word and then attempts to be clever in arguing about what they read there, they engage in willful disobedience. All the clever contortions of logic and witty sarcasm in the world will ring terrifyingly hollow when they stand in the presence of Almighty God to answer for their rebellion.

God is sovereign
Some things are not mine or yours to know; only human pride keeps us from accepting that.

*"**14** What shall we say then? Is there injustice on God's part? By no means! **15** For he says to Moses, "I will have mercy on whom I have mercy, and I will have compassion on whom I have compassion." **16** So then it depends not on human will or exertion, but on God, who has mercy. **17***

> *For the Scripture says to Pharaoh, "For this very purpose I have raised you up, that I might show my power in you, and that my name might be proclaimed in all the earth."* ***18*** *So then he has mercy on whomever he wills, and he hardens whomever he wills.*
>
> ***19*** *You will say to me then, "Why does he still find fault? For who can resist his will?"* ***20*** *But who are you, O man, to answer back to God? Will what is molded say to its molder, 'Why have you made me like this?'* ***21*** *Has the potter no right over the clay, to make out of the same lump one vessel for honorable use and another for dishonorable use?"*
> *– Romans 9:14-21*

There is one God

God has been clear that He is the only acceptable subject of worship for His creation.

> *"And God spoke all these words, saying, 2 'I am the Lord your God, who brought you out of the land of Egypt, out of the house of slavery. 3 You shall have no other gods before me.'"*
> *– Exodus 20:1-3*

When Jesus rebuked Satan, he reinforced the exclusive nature of our worship to God Almighty.

> *"...You shall worship the Lord your God and him only shall you serve."*
> *– Matthew 4:10*

Jesus also made it clear that He was the exclusive path to the Father.

> *"Jesus said to him, "I am the way, and the truth, and the life.* **No one comes to the Father except through me."**
> *– John 14:6 (emphasis mine)*

CHAPTER 8:
BASED ON WHAT?

Once one has determined that they are never too far away from God to turn back to him and that as long as one is alive, one can choose to turn to God, the first question is, who is the God we are discussing?

Many raised in Christian societies snort and are dismissive of this question, but even among those professing to be Christians, the question needs to be contemplated.

If we are talking about the God described in the Bible, where should we learn about Him and His wishes for us?

How strictly should we pay attention to what the almighty creator of the universe has communicated to us about his desires and preferences?

Is the Bible just a "jumping off point" for defining our beliefs and practices, or is it a strictly limited and exhaustive instruction manual for serving God?

One's answer to that question determines their beliefs, actions, and life decisions.

Effectively, one's attitude toward the Bible drives how one answers the second question that needs to be asked when turning (back) to God: "How do I know what God wants me to do?"

Many have been conditioned to turn to organized religions, churches, or learned religious leaders to ask what they need to do to be saved, but that is NOT what God has told us to do in His word.

You can figure it out for yourself

As noted earlier, in Philippians 2:12, Paul exhorts the faithful in Philippi to "...work out your own salvation with fear and trembling..."

"Work out your own salvation" does not tell them that they "earn" salvation, nor is it telling them to go out and make things up. It emphasizes that they have an active role in accessing God's grace. They aren't going to drift into salvation; they must work to learn God's will and submit to it.

"Ask, seek, knock" promise.

When Jesus says in Matthew 7:7-8, *"Ask, and it will be given to you; seek, and you will find; knock, and it will be opened to you.* **8** *For everyone who asks receives, and the one who seeks finds, and to the one who knocks it will be opened."* there is no hedging or half-stepping done. It is a simple promise that salvation is accessible if we are willing to pursue it.

Other writers have spoken of an increasing level of urgency in the actions described: ask (passive), seek (active), and knock (urgent). I don't know how much emphasis to put on that, but I think that the critical take-away is the absolute nature of the promise… "…it shall…", "…ye shall…", and "…it shall…" are definite promises.

> *"…it is impossible for God to lie,…"*
> *– Hebrews 6:18*

God can't lie, and He is faithful to His promises. Our willingness to hear, accept, and obey the answer to our questions is the variable that determines our salvation.

God communicates His will to us through the Bible. We will not find God's will by studying nature, as remarkable a testament to His grandeur it may be.

We must go to God's word. Other translations use the word "study" instead of "do your best" in 2 Timothy 2:15, but "rightly handling the word of truth" conveys that as well.

> *Do your best to present yourself to God as one approved, a worker who has no need to be ashamed, rightly handling the word of truth.*
> *– 2 Timothy 2:15*

Christianity in hostile times

> *"Blessed are you when others revile you and persecute you and utter all kinds of evil against you falsely on my account."*
> *– Matthew 5:11*

Paul instructs us to be at peace with all men in the Book of Romans. However, as society descends further and further into evil, instances will multiply, and Christians will stand out because they adhere to absolute truths. We must maintain the proper attitude and behavior in these circumstances, but Jesus has anticipated them and has described us as blessed for faithfully enduring these abuses.

> *"If possible, so far as it depends on you, live peaceably with all."*
> *– Romans 12:18*

The peace we are to maintain is not achieved through surrender to evil or silence in the face of error. As we grow in our faith, we have Biblical examples of sharing the reason for our hope (as I am in this book) with others. But our demeanor and approach must always be with the intent to persuade and save and never just to win an argument. If you think about it, that last approach is more about self and less about God. When confronted about that, the natural reaction is to assert some higher intent to defend truth boldly, but if untrue, God will hold you accountable for any damage your self-serving pride causes.

Satan uses pride and ego to corrupt noble intentions and then uses the noble intention to try to deflect accountability for the lack of agape in the action. It is up to us to always be on guard and monitor our motives.

I've discovered that, for the most part, the thing that jumps first to mind and that would feel the most satisfying to say is the wrong thing. I'm sure that's just a product of my frailties, but if you find it true, know you are not alone.

> *"Let your speech always be gracious, seasoned with salt, so that you may know how you ought to answer each person."*
> *– Colossians 4:6*

A gracious answer may take an extra beat to formulate, so it is wise to slow down your responses when a conversation becomes... challenging. If you find yourself getting angry, examine why. If it is because you are being asked a question for which you do not have a scriptural answer, be grateful for the indicator of an area of growth. Again, the goal is not to win an argument.

> *"Know this, my beloved brothers: let every person be quick to hear, slow to speak, slow to anger;* **20** *for the anger of man does not produce the righteousness of God."*
> *– James 1:19-20*

Regardless of how we are treated, we must remain faithful to God's word and only offer His revealed will as a reason for our actions. Our goal is not to inflame but to enlighten; God will assess the words we choose and the spirit with which we choose them.

> *"I tell you, on the day of judgment people will give account for every careless word they speak,* **37** *for by your words you will be justified, and by your words, you will be condemned."*
> *– Matthew 12:36-37*

Regardless of how carefully we choose our words, some will still want to force us to submit to their perspective and preferences, and our response must remain the same as that of Peter and the apostles:

> *"But Peter and the apostles answered, 'We must obey God rather than men.'"*
> *– Acts 5:29*

And we must be ready to accept adverse reactions and maintain a righteous demeanor.

We must be mentally prepared for the instances when someone becomes irritated or angry and starts to escalate the tone of the conversation into an argument. We must fight the urge to reflect the combativeness and maintain our focus on finding God's truth in the matter. We cannot let our reaction be the thing that stands between the listener and the truth.

> *"You have heard that it was said, 'An eye for an eye and a tooth for a tooth.' **39** But I say to you, Do not resist the one who is evil. But if anyone slaps you on the right cheek, turn to him the other also."*
> *– Matthew 5:38-39*

We must be cautious when we are confronted with the world's sinfulness. It is entirely appropriate to be revolted by the sinful acts we encounter and to be fearful of the horrible nature of the abominations that mankind so gleefully commits in the presence of the almighty creator of the universe.

But while Jesus, as God on Earth, demonstrated God's anger to the moneychangers in the Temple, we, as God's creation, are not given that right. We are to try to communicate the danger to anyone who will listen, but when we feel anger, it is almost always a sign that we need to get on our knees and pray for our own souls' condition and ask the Lord to help us restore the agape love into our hearts that we need.

CHAPTER 9:
HOW DO YOU HANDLE SCRIPTURE?

The Bible is sufficient.

The God who could speak our universe into existence could certainly communicate His wishes to us. An in-depth examination of the changing way God has interacted with humankind is beyond the scope of this effort. What matters to us, now, is that God's perfect revelation of His will ["...the perfect..." of 1 Corinthians 13:10] is available to us in the Bible. When people lose track of God's infallibility and omnipotence, they open themselves up to the idea that there must be subsequent or "clarifying" revelations. God anticipated that and covered it in His word. There is no need for any supplement to the Bible.

> "...contend for the faith that was once for all delivered to the saints."
> – Jude 1:3

As noted earlier, "once" indicates it was a singular occurrence. The phrase "...for all..." tells us the Bible's revelation is all-encompassing and eternal.

Going beyond the Bible is prohibited. God doesn't provide any leeway for adding or modifying His word. He doesn't need "help." He made us.

Humanity is often boldly arrogant in its ignorance of how truly microscopic our perspective on our existence in this earthly realm is. Their attitude is that in the two thousand years since the new covenant was shared, humanity has "evolved" in ways the Almighty couldn't anticipate. This sad perspective is only possible when God's scope of existence vs man's scope of existence is ignored.

> *"But do not overlook this one fact, beloved, that with the Lord one day is as a thousand years and a thousand years as one day."*
> *– 2 Peter 3:8*

> *"Everyone who goes on ahead and does not abide in the teaching of Christ, does not have God. Whoever abides in the teaching has both the Father and the Son."*
> *– 2 John 1:9*

This passage leaves no room for supplemental revelations or additions to what is expected of Biblical Christians. Choosing to adopt those additions means that the god who you are worshipping is not the God of the Bible.

For those who want to only submit to the direct utterances of Jesus (denoted with red ink in some Bibles), I direct you to the "givens" listed at the beginning of this book. What we have received as our "scripture" has been collected and passed down through centuries. If you believe in an omnipotent, omniscient, sovereign, and eternal God, then you believe that He controlled what we have received as our New Testament and that it contains everything we need to ask, seek, and knock. Choosing to "edit" that collection should make you tremble if you truly understand who God is.

Direct verbal inspiration

> *"All Scripture is breathed out by God and profitable for teaching, for reproof, for correction, and for training in righteousness, **17** that the man of God may be **complete**, equipped for **every good work**."*
> – 2 Timothy 3:16-17 (emphasis mine)

> *"...knowing this first of all, that no prophecy of Scripture comes from someone's own interpretation. **21** For no prophecy was ever produced by the will of man, but men spoke from God as they were carried along by the Holy Spirit."*
> – 2 Peter 1:20-21

> *"And we impart this in words not taught by human wisdom but taught by the Spirit, interpreting spiritual truths to those who are spiritual."*
> – 2 Corinthians 2:13

> *"And when they bring you before the synagogues and the rulers and the authorities, do not be anxious about how you should defend yourself or what you should say, **12** for the Holy Spirit will teach you in that very hour what you ought to say."*
> – Luke 12:11-12

I've heard the point made that if the Holy Spirit provided word for word what they should say when they were before "...rulers, and the authorities..." it would certainly make sense that the Holy Spirit would provide them with the words when it came time to communicate God's will in writing for all future generations.

> *"Do your best to present yourself to God as one approved, a worker who has no need to be ashamed, rightly handling the word of truth."*
> *– 2 Timothy 2:15*

The dangers of human logic

In writing this section, I understand many will misrepresent what I'm about to say as a declaration of doctrine or binding requirements for a Christian to be acceptable.

I am not doing that. I present things that each Christian should consider and decide what path best represents bending our own will to God's revelation. As I have indicated, I believe God will judge us based on our condition of heart when making our decisions, and only God and the individual can know what that is.

Also, as I have already stated, you will not be judged by what is in this book. You will be judged by what is in the Bible. When in doubt, go there.

That said...

I firmly believe that employing human logic, choosing expedience as a justification, making assumptions, and using implications/inferences to justify decisions concerning how we serve God are dangerous tactics. Each Christian must read the word and decide for themselves.

The problem with most "named" religious groups is that our individual frames of reference are short, and over time, even those groups that claim to be strictly Biblically based develop traditions. Many begin to think of those traditions as "givens" and core parts of Biblical faith without ever re-examining their Biblical basis or acceptability. "The way things always have been" … isn't.

Questions about many of these traditional practices and attitudes are brushed aside with a condescending chuckle and excuses of "logic" or "expedience." Still, any practice that is traditional rather than strictly scriptural, in addition to potentially being displeasing to God, also introduces problems for which answers may be challenging to find in scripture.

The modern concept of a "church" has been influenced by Protestant church practices, which were, in turn, influenced by common practices and attitudes stemming from the Catholic Church.

> "Religion that is pure and undefiled before God the Father is this: to visit orphans and widows in their affliction, and to keep oneself unstained from the world."
> – James 1:27

There is a certain "Spiritual Inertia," a set of conclusions and opinions based on the "way we've always done it" that we all must fight to overcome in working out our salvation; it is difficult to change a lifelong perspective.

> **"...give thought to do what is honorable in the sight of all." – Romans 12:17**

Hearing people whine, "Don't judge me!" can be very tiring when they are discovered to have misbehaved. But as Christians, we are called upon to judge (discern) for our own lives what is acceptable to God and what behaviors will reflect the glory of God's influence in our lives.

The most important consideration for a Christian is what pleases God. Within that context, we must reflect God's influence in our lives. This should inspire us to avoid entanglements in any of the ever-present "grey area" situations that present themselves in business dealings, social interactions, etc. If a thing seems questionable, then a humble spirit will choose to serve God and not do the questionable thing.

We see people pretending to be vigorously presenting the word of God and using inflammatory language toward those who profess themselves to be Christians who believe differently. We see people who profess to be representing our Savior publicly burning books of other religions and attacking all who do not profess Christianity. While I agree that we are to proclaim the Truth boldly, I challenge all these individuals to explain how angering and antagonizing those with whom we disagree demonstrates agape. Does creating spiritual wounds open minds or close them? What is the goal of your speaking? To persuade people to consider Christ or to win an argument. If the belief is that a toxic attack on a non-believer somehow blesses onlookers, I struggle to accept it.

In our day-to-day interactions at work, what image of Christians are we leaving behind?

- Honest or "clever"?
- Patient or combative?
- Loving and merciful or able to hold a grudge for years?

It is very easy to get caught up in the heat of the moment or our pursuit of earthly goals and forget that the real reason behind all our efforts is serving God and our soul's salvation.

"Whatever you do, work heartily, as for the Lord and not for men,"
– Colossians 3:23

I submit that if we "work heartily, as unto the Lord," it will profoundly affect our interactions with co-workers and how we view our work.

We should consider all our actions in terms of whether they will make those observing them more or less likely to be willing to hear the truth from our lips.

Many will reject the truth, regardless of how it is presented. However, that does not relieve us of the responsibility to deliver the truth in an easily received manner and to represent Christianity positively.

Salvation in the "Wait... what?" moments

As we examine the scriptures, there is a good chance that at some point, we will encounter a passage that causes us to stop and think, "Wait, what?" because it doesn't seem to align with what we've always believed or been taught. This conflict may be due to taking a passage out of context or some other misunderstanding; however, our approach to dealing with this situation is critical in determining our success in seeking God.

Dismissing or ignoring the perceived disconnect between our perspective and what we read in God's word is either spiritual laziness or a subtle form of rebellion. The pure heart desiring to please God will embrace the issue and study it further to determine whether what was previously believed is scriptural.

An unexamined and untested faith is dangerous; Contrast the Bereans and those from Thessalonica.

> *"Now these Jews were more noble than those in Thessalonica; they received the word with all eagerness, examining the Scriptures daily to see if these things were so."*
> *– Acts 17:11*

1 Corinthians 13 shows us that mindless performance is useless, no matter how precise. It is pointless if our service is not motivated by love [agape]. We must always ensure that the reason behind our choice springs from a perspective of agape and is not just the result of spiritual inertia.

CHAPTER 10:
WHOSE OPINION MATTERS MORE?

"So, isn't believing in God and living a 'good life' enough?"

> *"At Caesarea there was a man named Cornelius, a centurion of what was known as the Italian Cohort,* **2** *a devout man who feared God with all his household, gave alms generously to the people, and prayed continually to God."*
> *– Acts 10:1-2*

Some seem to believe that all the details are not as important as just being a "good person" and not doing obviously bad (by society's standards) things. But in the story of Cornelius, we see a man who was described as "devout," "one who feared God," "who gave alms generously to the people," and "prayed continually to God." Even this devout man needed further instruction in God's will from Peter.

I had a conversation with a fellow once who considered himself a good person but didn't really get into "all that church stuff" and felt like God was somehow going to view his willful pursuit of his own path with a sort of grudging respect for him knowing "his own mind." There are few delusions that are more dangerous.

This mythical God who somehow respects rebellion is not found anywhere in the Bible. The God found there is one who had demonstrated the consequences of disobedience often enough for us to have no excuses for being unwilling to learn the lesson.

It is not "Hellfire and Brimstone" teaching to enumerate a few instances of divine punishment to ensure that the consequences of not humbling ourselves before God are made perfectly clear.

Uzzah

Many circumstances came together to create the situation in which Uzzah found himself. Still, God had specified how the ark of the covenant was to be handled, and Uzzah disobeyed those specifications, no matter what his intentions were.

> "And when they came to the threshing floor of Nacon, Uzzah put out his hand to the ark of God and took hold of it, for the oxen stumbled. 7 And the anger of the Lord was kindled against Uzzah, and God struck him down there because of his error, and he died there beside the ark of God."
> – 2 Samual 6:6-7

The whole tale of Uzzah is rife with indications of ignorance of God's will, leading to a tragic outcome. If we choose to serve God, we must actively learn His will for us.

Ananias and Sapphira

"But a man named Ananias, with his wife Sapphira, sold a piece of property, 2 and with his wife's knowledge he kept back for himself some of the proceeds and brought only a part of it and laid it at the apostles' feet. 3 But Peter said, 'Ananias, why has Satan filled your heart to lie to the Holy Spirit and to keep back for yourself part of the proceeds of the land? 4 While it remained unsold, did it not remain your own? And after it was sold, was it not at your disposal? Why is it that you have contrived this deed in your heart? You have not lied to man but to God.' 5 When Ananias heard these words, he fell down and breathed his last. And great fear came upon all who heard of it. 6 The young men rose and wrapped him up and carried him out and buried him.

7 After an interval of about three hours his wife came in, not knowing what had happened. 8 And Peter said to her, "Tell me whether you sold the land for so much." And she said, "Yes, for so much." 9 But Peter said to her, "How is it that you have agreed together to test the Spirit of the Lord? Behold, the feet of those who have buried your husband are at the door, and they will carry you out." 10 Immediately she fell down at his feet and breathed her last. When the young men came in they found her dead, and they carried her out and buried her beside her husband."
– Acts 5:1-10

God doesn't take disobedience lightly. Think about your life as that piece of land Ananias and Sapphira sold.

Do you think God will look favorably on your "hiding back" part of it?

Nadab and Abihu

> *"Now Nadab and Abihu, the sons of Aaron, each took his censer and put fire in it and laid incense on it and offered unauthorized fire before the Lord, which he had not commanded them. **2** And fire came out from before the Lord and consumed them, and they died before the Lord."*
> *– Leviticus 10:1-2*

God gave unambiguous instructions about how he was to be worshipped. Nadab and Abihu chose to worship God in a manner that differed from His instructions. God was not pleased.

When considering these three cases, Ananias and Sapphira are the least sympathetic characters because they were greedy and willing to lie to God's representative about it.

Nadab and Abihu appeared lazy; however, as God's representatives, they should have known better and acted with due respect.

Of the three, Uzzah comes closest to being a sympathetic character because it is easy to imagine the reflex of reaching out and steadying the most holy relic of Israel. There is even a reference made to David's disappointment at the outcome. However, God was very clear in His instructions about handling the Ark, and Uzzah should not have been able to touch it. The Ark was not supposed to be moved via cart, and violating this commandment put Uzzah in the position to make a fatal error.

CHAPTER 11:
ATTITUDE CHECK

Let's quickly check what God's word says on a few topics, and you can judge for yourself if any of these make you squirm. You won't be getting mad at me if you get mad at these passages.

Husbands and wives

"Wives, submit to your own husbands, as to the Lord. **23** *For the husband is the head of the wife even as Christ is the head of the church, his body, and is himself its Savior.* **24** *Now as the church submits to Christ, so also wives should submit in everything to their husbands."*
– Ephesians 5:22-24

"Likewise, wives, be subject to your own husbands, so that even if some do not obey the word, they may be won without a word by the conduct of their wives, **2** *when they see your*

*respectful and pure conduct. **3** Do not let your adorning be external—the braiding of hair and the putting on of gold jewelry, or the clothing you wear"*
– 1 Peter 3:1-3

"Wives, submit to your husbands, as is fitting in the Lord."
– Colossians 3:18

Homosexuality

The following two passages are from the Old Testament and, as such, are not "binding" on Christians as law; however, they describe homosexuality as an "abomination." The prohibition is repeated for Christians in the subsequent three passages.

"You shall not lie with a male as with a woman; it is an abomination."
– Leviticus 18:22

"If a man lies with a male as with a woman, both of them have committed an abomination; they shall surely be put to death; their blood is upon them."
– Leviticus 20:13

*"For this reason God gave them up to dishonorable passions. For their women exchanged natural relations for those that are contrary to nature; **27** and the men likewise gave up natural relations with women and were consumed with passion for one another, men committing shameless acts with men and receiving in themselves the due penalty for their error."*
– Romans 1:26-27

> "...just as Sodom and Gomorrah and the surrounding cities, which likewise indulged in sexual immorality and pursued unnatural desire, serve as an example by undergoing a punishment of eternal fire."
> – Jude 1:7

> "Or do you not know that the unrighteous will not inherit the kingdom of God? Do not be deceived: neither the sexually immoral, nor idolaters, nor adulterers, nor men who practice homosexuality, **10** nor thieves, nor the greedy, nor drunkards, nor revilers, nor swindlers will inherit the kingdom of God."
> – 1 Corinthians 6:9-10

Let's be clear here: I do not believe in a loving God who would put a soul on this earth, give them irresistible urges beyond what they could control, and then sit back and enjoy watching the miserable life that person leads.

I do believe that Satan has been allowed to tempt us with urges, but not beyond the point that we can resist them.

> "No temptation has overtaken you that is not common to man. God is faithful, and he will not let you be tempted beyond your ability, but with the temptation he will also provide the way of escape, that you may be able to endure it."
> – 1 Corinthians 10:13

I see nothing in scripture indicating that the consequences are more severe for pursuing one form of sexual disobedience to God's will than another form. Heterosexual fornication or adultery is not somehow "better" than homosexuality.

Exposing children to heterosexual smut is not somehow better than exposing them to homosexual or transgender smut, and God had very pointed warnings about misleading little ones.

> *"And calling to him a child, he put him in the midst of them 3 and said, "Truly, I say to you, unless you turn and become like children, you will never enter the kingdom of heaven. 4 Whoever humbles himself like this child is the greatest in the kingdom of heaven.*
>
> *5 "Whoever receives one such child in my name receives me, 6 but whoever causes one of these little ones who believe in me to sin, it would be better for him to have a great millstone fastened around his neck and to be drowned in the depth of the sea."*
> *— Matthew 18:2-6*

Transsexuality

This is another abomination to the Lord that has become widely accepted in modern society. (Again, this is from the Old Law and is not binding; however, the description as an "abomination" is significant.)

> *"A woman shall not wear a man's garment, nor shall a man put on a woman's cloak, for whoever does these things is an abomination to the Lord your God."*
> *— Deuteronomy 22:5*

God isn't the source of the confusion.

> "But from the beginning of creation, 'God made them male and female.'"
> – Mark 10:6

In another context, Jesus said to the Pharisees...

> "...For what is exalted among men is an abomination in the sight of God."
> – Luke 16:15

... but it applies here. Returning to the fundamental issue of humbling our will to God and working out our own salvation, it must be asked... Is engaging in something God has ever described as an "abomination" something that demonstrates humbling ourselves to His will?

Women in leadership positions in the church

> "...the women should keep silent in the churches. For they are not permitted to speak, but should be in submission, as the Law also says. **35** If there is anything they desire to learn, let them ask their husbands at home. For it is shameful for a woman to speak in church."
> – 1 Corinthians 14:34-35

Subjection to governmental authority

Rebellion against God's will comes in many forms. God's command to submit to the (often corrupt) earthly governments can chafe and create a temptation to rebel, but God's word is unambiguous.

> "Let every person be subject to the governing authorities. For there is no authority except from God, and those that

*exist have been instituted by God. **2** Therefore whoever resists the authorities resists what God has appointed, and those who resist will incur judgement. **3** For rulers are not a terror to good conduct, but to bad. Would you have no fear of the one who is in authority? Then do what is good, and you will receive his approval, **4** for he is God's servant for your good. But if you do wrong, be afraid, for he does not bear the sword in vain. For he is the servant of God, an avenger who carries out God's wrath on the wrongdoer. **5** Therefore, one must be in subjection, not only to avoid God's wrath but also for the sake of conscience. **6** For because of this you also pay taxes, for the authorities are ministers of God, attending to this very thing. **7** Pay to all what is owed to them: taxes to whom taxes are owed, revenue to whom revenue is owed, respect to whom respect is owed, honor to whom honor is owed."*
– Romans 13:1-7

I confess I stumble when I read "...*and those that exist have been instituted by God...*" But as evil as our government has become, we must remember that the first-century Christians reading this were under Roman rule. We have nothing to complain about by comparison.

Infinite forgiveness

Jesus tells us to forgive "seventy-seven times" (infinitely). Ask yourself, how easy will it be to forgive the third time... really? Is there someone from years ago whose memory still makes you clench just a little? God's will is that we let that go. It is not easy. Pray about it.

"Then Peter came up and said to him, "Lord, how often will my brother sin against me, and I forgive him? As many as

seven times?" **22** Jesus said to him, "I do not say to you seven times, but seventy-seven times."
– Matthew 18:21-22

"To one who strikes you on the cheek, offer the other also, and from one who takes away your cloak do not withhold your tunic either."
– Luke 6:29

I confess that the challenge of this passage humbles me. To have submitted to God's will to the extent that if someone steals something from me, I offer them more?

Marriage & divorce

"It was also said, 'Whoever divorces his wife, let him give her a certificate of divorce.' **32** But I say to you that everyone who divorces his wife, except on the ground of sexual immorality, makes her commit adultery, and whoever marries a divorced woman commits adultery."
– Matthew 5:31-32

"And he said to them, 'Whoever divorces his wife and marries another commits adultery against her, **12** and if she divorces her husband and marries another, she commits adultery.'"
– Mark 10:11-12

"Everyone who divorces his wife and marries another commits adultery, and he who marries a woman divorced from her husband commits adultery."
– Luke 16:18

I tried to offer limited commentary on these passages because my thoughts are irrelevant. What is relevant is your reaction. If you can read through all of these and seriously ponder the implications without feeling challenged by any of them, I salute you. If any of them make you angry, be aware that you are not angry at me because I didn't write these words. These words are the words of God, and if you are unwilling to bend to His will, you are making a choice.

If the god who you worship condones anything different than what is included in these passages, you are not worshipping the God of the Bible. God hasn't included "optional" sections in His revelation. While he has made grace available to us to serve as a "bridge" between what we can do with our sincerest efforts and the requirements of a perfect standard, I see nothing to indicate that grace is intended to cover willful disobedience.

> *"What shall we say then? Are we to continue in sin that grace may abound? **2** By no means! How can we who died to sin still live in it?"*
> *– Romans 6:1-2*

The God who created us made us with free will, so I certainly cannot stop you from worshipping a god of your own creation. But I want to make sure that you are aware of your conscious decision to do so. And make no mistake about it: consciously choosing to ignore and disobey any portion of God's new covenant with us means you are defining a different god to worship.

CHAPTER 12:
THE BELIEVER'S FOUNDATION

Among those claiming to be Christians, there are five main perspectives:

1) There are those who have confidence and peace of mind because of a knowledge of God's will.
These Christians have studied God's word and set out to arrange their lives and priorities in a way pleasing to God.

2) There are those who have confidence and peace of mind because of an ignorance of God's will. There is no such thing as "innocent ignorance" because God has put the responsibility squarely on the shoulders of everyone to "work out your own salvation." These Christians have let someone else tell them about God and what they think God expects of His creation. This category would also include those who have tried to figure

it out themselves but have allowed their personal preferences to stand between them and the truth. At the very least, these Christians are in a dangerous situation because, again, they have ignored the exhortation in Philippians 2:12 to *"...work out your own salvation with fear and trembling;"*

Worst case, these Christians have "church shopped" until they found someone that would tell them what they wanted to hear.

"For the time is coming when people will not endure sound teaching, but having itching ears they will accumulate for themselves teachers to suit their own passions, 4 and will turn away from listening to the truth and wander off into myths."
– 2 Timothy 4:3-

The teachers who mislead these poor folks will bear a heavy responsibility of their own in the judgment as detailed in James 3:1...

"Not many of you should become teachers, my brothers, for you know that we who teach will be judged with greater strictness."
– James 3:1

3) There are those who have anxiety because of an ignorance of God's grace and his will.

   These Christians have often been indoctrinated with the "gospel" of "everything is not enough" by a cult of inadequacy that claims to be encouraging Christians to be diligent and to run the race as though only one might win when, in reality, the focus is a dismissal and neglect of the gift of grace that God has offered to us to make our yoke easy and our burden light. The truth is that while we are to give our all to God, God knows our hearts and will judge us on that, not on a points system attached to works.

4) There are those who have anxiety because of a knowledge of God's will.

Closely related to the previous group, these Christians know God's will but have not decided to submit to it completely. Often, the cares of the world... the job, school, hobbies, friends, etc.- distract from a total commitment to God. The knowledge of their lack of commitment nags at their conscience and denies them peace of mind, in this case, due to a properly functioning conscience.

5) There are those who have peace of mind because they don't care about God's will.

I include this group because of the way I framed the category... "...those claiming to be Christians..." but the reality is that these folks have so little regard for the Bible that applying the name "Christian" to them is a questionable usage of language. They worship a god so limited that he doesn't understand man's capacity for growth and change and, therefore, must accept whatever this "changed man" chooses to offer up as worship and respect whatever abominable behavior this "changed man" chooses to call acceptable. These people have created an avatar or idol for their rebellion and called it "God," but it is in no way related to the God described in the Bible.

Another slight variation on this persona is represented by people who have let their earthly pride so dominate their perspective that they develop this misguided notion that God somehow respects their rebelliousness. Their ignorance of the nature of God has allowed them to dream that God somehow looks admiringly on them as being a "Man's Man." God does not respect or tolerate Man's Men... He is looking for God's Men.

The Bible is the only way we know God's will.
The Bible never entertains any concept of "flexibility" regarding its authority. No concept is taught of "start here and then explore other human authors' works for a fuller understanding." The Bible itself is inflexible and autocratic, and if you are uncomfortable with that idea, you are not uncomfortable with me or my "interpretation." It is the God of the Bible's explicitly communicated will against which you are rebelling.

In his letter to the Galatians, Paul plainly states that God's will is only found in the truths he and the other Apostles taught.

> *"But even if we or an angel from heaven should preach to you a gospel contrary to the one we preached to you, let him be accursed. 9 As we have said before, so now I say again: If anyone is preaching to you a gospel contrary to the one you received, let him be accursed."*
> *– Galatians 1:8-9*

All the Bible is God's word.

> *"All Scripture is breathed out by God and profitable for teaching, for reproof, for correction, and for training in righteousness, **17** that the man of God may be complete, equipped for every good work."*
> – 2 Timothy 3:16-17

The Old Testament is not a binding covenant on Christians.
While every scripture is "profitable for teaching, for reproof, for correction, for instruction which is in righteousness," not all scripture communicates binding commandments for Christians.

The Old Testament is the source of knowledge of the God we worship, His nature, and His relationship with His creation. The Old Testament communicated a binding law on the Children of Israel, and while it still provides insight into God's nature and His relationships with man, it is not binding on Christians as law.

Christians do not observe the Sabbath (Saturday) as a holy day, we do not abstain from shellfish and pork as a matter of faith, and we do not practice circumcision as an act of worship, among other differences.

Acts 15:1-21 – When certain Judaeans came down teaching that Gentile converts had to be circumcised and observe the Old Law (the law of Moses found in the Old Testament), Paul and Barnabus and other Christians went to Jerusalem to ask the apostles and elders. In Jerusalem, Peter and James indicated that the Old Law did not bind Gentiles.

*"Therefore let no one pass judgement on you in questions of food and drink, or with regard to a festival or a new moon or a Sabbath. **17** These are a shadow of the things to come, but the substance belongs to Christ. **18** Let no one disqualify you, insisting on asceticism and worship of angels, going on in detail about visions, puffed up without reason by his sensuous mind, **19** and not holding fast to the Head, from whom the whole body, nourished and knit together through its joints and ligaments, grows with a growth that is from God. **20** If with Christ you died to the elemental spirits of the world, why, as if you were still alive in the world, do you submit to regulations— **21** 'Do not handle, Do not taste, Do not touch' **22** (referring to things that all perish as they are used)— according to human precepts and teachings? **23** These have indeed an appearance of wisdom in promoting self-made religion and asceticism and severity to the body, but they are of no value in stopping the indulgence of the flesh."*
– Colossians 2:16-23

Romans 14 discusses the challenges that Jews faced as the Old Law was being replaced by the New Testament and they transitioned their practices to the perfect law of liberty.

Galatians

Much of the book of Galatians deals with Paul addressing the issue of those who had received the gospel clinging to the Old Law and not fully embracing the perfect law of liberty. While the first-century church understandably had to work through this transition, we have no such excuse today. We have the complete revelation of the new covenant to guide our journey to God.

Hebrews

The writer of the Book of Hebrews explains that the Old Law had been replaced with the New Testament.

> *"For if that first covenant had been faultless, there would have been no occasion to look for a second.* **8** *For he finds fault with them when he says: 'Behold, the days are coming, declares the Lord, when I will establish a new covenant with the house of Israel and with the house of Judah,* **9** *not like the covenant that I made with their fathers on the day when I took them by the hand to bring them out of the land of Egypt. For they did not continue in my covenant, and so I showed no concern for them, declares the Lord.* **10** *For this is the covenant that I will make with the house of Israel after those days, declares the Lord: I will put my laws into their minds, and write them on their hearts, and I will be their God, and they shall be my people.* **11** *And they shall not teach, each one his neighbor and each one his brother, saying, 'Know the Lord,' for they shall all know me, from the least of them to the greatest.* **12** *For I will be merciful toward their iniquities, and I will remember their sins no more.'* **13** *In speaking of a new covenant, he makes the first one obsolete. And what is becoming obsolete and growing old is ready to vanish away."*
> – Hebrews 8:7-13

The New Testament is the complete description of God's will

There is no room for "additions" to the New Testament, and the promises clearly attach to staying within its teachings.

> "Everyone who goes on ahead and does not abide in the teaching of Christ, does not have God. Whoever abides in the teaching has both the Father and the Son."
> – 2 John 1:9

God doesn't change; Therefore, God's will for us doesn't change

There is this notion that man has "evolved" since the New Testament was given, and it is born of humanity's limited concept of time and the impression that it has been SO long since the New Testament was revealed. As mentioned earlier, the two thousand years since the revelation of the new covenant between God and man is nothing to God.

> "But do not overlook this one fact, beloved, that with the Lord one day is as a thousand years, and a thousand years as one day."
> – 2 Peter 3:8

> "...contend for the faith that was **once for all** delivered to the saints."
> – Jude 1:3 (emphasis mine)

The phrase "once for all" doesn't leave room for an "evolving" faith. A finality and a completeness are communicated there that cannot safely be dismissed.

There will be consequences for unrepentant rebellion

> "Everyone who goes on ahead and does not abide in the teaching of Christ, does not have God. Whoever abides in the teaching has both the Father and the Son."
> – 2 John 1:9

The warning here is obvious, and the choice it leaves is just as clear. Follow ("abide in") the teaching of Christ or don't. But don't kid yourself about whether there will be consequences.

Satan wants you ignorant

Some religious organizations have pursued a strategy of keeping their followers ignorant of God's word, in extreme cases, by limiting access to the scriptures. In modern times, the far more common approach is not encouraging people to read the Bible for themselves.

By encouraging people just to let preachers, scholars, and priests "interpret" God's will for them, any number of completely un-Biblical practices can be promoted by emphasizing cultural norms, pseudo-science, and human logic.

Again, God, who we only know about because of the Bible, told us what He wanted from us… in the Bible. The path to God involves reading, praying, believing, and submitting to God's will. It is straightforward, but as we have all learned, simple does not imply easy.

We must be cautious in evaluating the motives of those offering spiritual guidance. One of the most insidious tools that Satan uses on most of us is the temptation to judge those around us based on our limited observations of their behavior and the arrogant delusion that we know "why" someone else does something or says something. We form conclusions without knowing everything that has happened in their lives or is currently happening or their true motivations, and we are frequently very wrong.

However, observed behaviors do provide clues about people's priorities and nature. As Matthew tells us…

> "You will recognize them by their fruits. Are grapes gathered from thornbushes, or figs from thistles? **17** So, every healthy tree bears good fruit, but the diseased tree bears bad fruit. **18** A healthy tree cannot bear bad fruit, nor can a diseased tree bear good fruit. **19** Every tree that does not bear good fruit is cut down and thrown into the fire. **20** Thus you will recognize them by their fruits."
> – Matthew 7:16-20

This being the case, it is essential, in deciding with whom one will discuss Biblical matters, to observe their reaction when questioned about something they practice, believe, or teach. A true Christian, being aware of our fallible nature and desiring, more than anything else, to be pleasing to God, will welcome an honest and open investigation and engage in the discussion happily as long as all parties listen and honestly evaluate the beliefs expressed.

As we mentioned in the beginning, while we each have our own salvation to work out, we also have a responsibility to share the Good News with as many others as possible. But be prepared to encounter individuals with a vested interest in the status quo who will not discuss to understand, but dispute. Because we are not omniscient and cannot see into their hearts, unfortunately, a certain amount of time must be invested in reaching even the most closed-off hearts because that is the nature of agape.

However, when it becomes clear that it has turned into a debate vs. a search for the truth, it is best to move along to try to find a soul who is genuinely searching for the truth rather than "casting your pearls before swine."

"Do not give dogs what is holy, and do not throw your pearls before pigs, lest they trample them underfoot and turn to attack you."
– Matthew 7:6

We are not here to "win arguments" but to find and help the lost.

Truth

One of the more tiresome idiocies in modern society is the ridiculous assertion that there is no absolute truth and that anything you believe is "your truth."

In their excellent book, "I Don't Have Enough Faith to be an Atheist," Geisler and Turek do such an entertaining and compelling job of dealing with this nonsense from a logical perspective that I will not attempt to go down that path here. I highly recommend their book for that chapter alone, if no other. It is a brilliant piece of work.

However, if we claim to worship "the God of the Bible," then we must know what the God of the Bible says about Himself.

Jesus claimed to be "the truth."

> *"Jesus said to him, "I am the way, and **the truth**, and the life. No one comes to the Father except through me."*
> *– John 14:6 (emphasis mine)*

Jesus described the Holy Spirit as "the Spirit of truth."

> *"And I will ask the Father, and he will give you another Helper to be with you forever, **17** even the Spirit of truth, whom the*

world cannot receive, because it neither sees him nor knows him. You know him, for he dwells with you and will be in you."
— John 14:16-17

Paul refers to God as being unable to lie.

"...in hope of eternal life, which God, who never lies, promised before the ages began"
— Titus 1:2

There is only one "truth."

It doesn't matter who is telling you otherwise. They are wrong. That's MY "truth." However, despite how passionately and firmly I believe it, that statement represents my BELIEF about the situation, and I cannot authoritatively assert anything different through the force of my intellect.

Multiple beliefs can exist about a topic, but I submit that there is only one truth. Some beliefs may be closer to the truth than others, but there is no guarantee that they are even remotely close.

Beliefs based on partial truths or misapplication of truths lead to error. We discussed the dangers of an overreliance on human logic earlier. Satan employed a misapplication of truth in his temptation of Jesus. This is a reminder that statements that are true in and of themselves always need to be evaluated in a broader context. A properly applied truth will never conflict with another truth in God's revelation.

We are blessed to have THE truth to use as a measuring stick in this situation.

> *"Jesus said to him, "**I** am the way, and **the truth**, and the life. No one comes to the Father except through me."*
> *– John 14:6 (emphasis mine)*

Jesus doesn't leave room for negotiation or misinterpretation with his declaration: "*I am **the** way, and **the** truth, and **the** life...*" [emphasis mine]. He did not say "I am **a** way, and **a** truth, and **a** life...," but **the** (exclusive, singular, unique) way.

> *"... and you will know **the truth**, and **the truth** will set you free."*
> *– John 8:32 (emphasis mine)*

Once again, Jesus doesn't leave any room for misunderstanding. They were going to know "the truth," and "**the** truth" would free them.

So, if there is a singular ("the") truth, where can it be found? Jesus answered that in his prayer to God for his disciples.

> *"Sanctify them in **the truth; your word is truth**."*
> *– John 17:17 (emphasis mine)*

God has made it clear that He wants us to be at peace with all men [Romans 12:18], but not at the expense of truth. He has shared the truth with us, and He wants no compromise.

Biblical authority spectrum

I wanted to do a graphical representation of the range of attitudes people had about the authority of the Bible. An interesting clarification occurred while building the "Biblical Authority Spectrum." Having built a few presentations in my time, I wanted to space the labels around the "danger gauge" (something like the gas gauge in old cars...

"Empty" to "Full") to balance the image. However, I realized that our attitudes about the exclusive authority of the Bible, while possibly varying in intensity, really break out into two possible conditions. We either have the appropriate respect for God's word and handle it accordingly, or we don't.

People's attitudes about the Bible usually fall somewhere on a spectrum ranging from "Infallible Word of God" to "Evil Manifesto for Male Dominance."

Those who believe the Bible is God's infallible word tend to take its contents seriously and carefully study it to learn God's will for His creation.

An attitude that the Bible is anything less than the infallible word of God will tend to inspire people to feel free to pick and choose what portions to follow and what portions to ignore.

This makes it very tough to focus on the loving aspects of our creator because before the focus is shifted to God's love, there first needs to be an appropriate reverence and respect for his dominion. However, somehow, over the years, as we have lost a general societal awareness of the contents of God's word, our awareness of the awesome grandeur and worshipful majesty of our creator has been lost and replaced with this weak-willed, indulgent entity that will accept whatever scraps of our lives we want to offer Him.

So, before truly appreciating God's love, we must understand the "fire and brimstone" alternative. We must humble ourselves before Him and submit our will to His dominion, not try to dictate to Him what He will get from us as an offering.

CHAPTER 13:
PEACE AND CONFIDENCE IN THE END

Callused knees are a good start

The fact that you are bothering to read this book is a good sign because it means you are searching. The humility to know that you need something is critical to finding the path to salvation.

The "Ask, Seek, Knock" promise is a powerful and comforting passage to those searching. God guarantees that we will find the path to Him if we sincerely look for it.

> *"Ask, and it will be given to you; seek, and you will find; knock, and it will be opened to you."*
> *– Matthew 7:7*

I bring this passage up repeatedly because it is crucial to understanding how much God wants us to succeed in finding Him. There is no hedging or qualifying of the promise here. However, the clear embedded qualification is that we are asking with the intent of listening to His answer, seeking with the intent of taking up whatever truth we find and knocking with the intent of going in through whatever door opens.

I cannot know how sincere anyone else's quest for the truth is. God does. All I can do is learn what God has revealed and then submit to it.

When we are truly aware of the unmerited gift of God's grace, we are inspired to pray sincere prayers of gratitude and praise and to approach others who may have wandered with humility.

People's attitudes about God's expectations for us seem to range from "No mistakes allowed" to "Anything goes." I believe that the truth lies somewhere in between. While I know that perfection was attainable by only one born of woman (Jesus), I do believe that our love for God is demonstrated by how seriously we handle His instruction.

The problem is that so many of us who believe in reading God's word and trying to follow it have focused so much on doctrinal precision that they have developed a dismissive attitude about all discussions about grace. When grace is brought up, it is immediately met with, "Yeah, but…" and then a long recitation of every passage that describes the consequences of rebellion and sin.

Over time, this focus on consequences and our shortcomings and failures breed a toxic uncertainty that Satan welcomes and uses to discourage us and try to make us give up. In young, undeveloped

Christians, it often leads to abandoning what is perceived as a hopeless pursuit.

Indeed, the New Testament encourages us to live with the intensity of runners in a race where only one can win the prize.

> *"Do you not know that in a race all the runners run, but only one receives the prize? So run that you may obtain it. **25** Every athlete exercises self-control in all things. They do it to receive a perishable wreath, but we an imperishable. **26** So I do not run aimlessly; I do not box as one beating the air. **27** But I discipline my body and keep it under control, lest after preaching to others I myself should be disqualified."*
> *– 1 Corinthians 9:24-27*

But again, that same New Testament has PROMISED us that we can find our way to Him. Reread it:

> *"Ask, and it will be given to you; seek, and you will find; knock, and it will be opened to you."*
> *– Matthew 7:7*

And that same New Testament has also promised that we won't be tempted beyond what we can handle.

> *"No temptation has overtaken you that is not common to man. God is faithful, and he will not let you be tempted beyond your ability, but with the temptation he will also provide the way of escape, that you may be able to endure it."*
> *– 1 Corinthians 10:13*

"Whittlin' on God's end of the stick"

Growing up as a preacher's kid, I was introduced to many of my dad's contemporaries, many of whom were Biblical scholars and fine Gospel ministers. But my favorite was a preacher from Burnet, TX, named Robert Turner. Brother Turner could turn complex situations into relatable language like none other, and one of my favorites of his creations was his description of our tendency to meddle in God's affairs as "whittlin' on God's end of the stick."

I've thought about it, and my interpretation of the phrase goes something like this:

- There are things that God has told me
- There are things that God has not told me
- There are things that don't fit my earthly concept of "fairness."

But:

- "His ways are not my ways..." so I need to accept His dominion and leave "fairness" up to him.

"For my thoughts are not your thoughts,
neither are your ways my ways, declares the Lord.
9 *For as the heavens are higher than the earth,*
so are my ways higher than your ways
and my thoughts than your thoughts."
– Isaiah 55:8-9

People can "whittle on God's end of the stick" about contentious concepts until Judgement Day. Still, based on what has been revealed in God's word, it is fair to believe that if something matters to how we live our lives in service to God, it has been revealed clearly and without ambiguity. Based on the "Ask, Seek, Knock" promise previously referenced, I believe that.

What is left is to work with the revealed truths, avoid the unrevealed truths, and pray in faith, remembering the "Ask, Seek, Knock" promise.

In matters of uncertainty, the "tie" should be decided by agape (love).

"Whittlin' on God's end of the stick" manifests itself in other ways as well, and one of the most destructive ways is the tendency of some Christians to make a personal decision on a spiritual matter (usually by employing the "logic" previously discussed) and then try to bind their decision on other Christians. This goes WAY beyond personal discernment and crosses right over into the realm of adding to God's revelation and "judgment," which is God's end of the stick.

"Seek ye first the Kingdom…"

One of Satan's most effective tools for distracting us is his ability to take something that is a legitimate earthly pursuit and get us to over-emphasize it to the neglect of our soul's well-being. For example, we need to provide for ourselves and our families, but it is very easy to get so focused on that effort that we lose focus on serving God and pleasing Him.

Our earthly needs are tangible, immediate, and measurable, and our spiritual needs are in the realm of faith. It is very easy to get distracted, and we must constantly be on our guard to prioritize what is truly important.

*"But godliness with contentment is great gain, **7** for we brought nothing into the world, and we cannot take anything out of the world. **8** But if we have food and clothing, with these we will be content. **9** But those who desire to be rich fall into temptation, into a snare, into many senseless and harmful desires that plunge people into ruin and destruction. **10** For the love of money is a root of all kinds of evils. It is through this craving that some have wandered away from the faith and pierced themselves with many pangs." – 1 Timothy 6:6-10*

CHAPTER 14:
ASK, SEEK, KNOCK

Much of what has been discussed to this point has been about God's omnipotence and His trustworthiness. That combination makes the "Ask, Seek, Knock" promise a powerful one. Because it is so powerful, I want to leave you with a final look at it.

> *"Ask, and it will be given to you; seek, and you will find; knock, and it will be opened to you."*
> *– Matthew 7:7*

Consider the absolute nature of this promise. "...it shall be given", "...ye shall find", "...it shall be opened." Nothing tempers these promises. God Almighty has PROMISED you that if you ask, seek, and knock sincerely, you CAN find Him and His Truth, and God can't lie.

> *"...it is impossible for God to lie..."*
> *– Hebrews 6:18*

This has a couple of interesting implications that I want you to consider. If, given these promises, one encounters a problem that seems unsolvable scripturally... to fellowship, not to fellowship, to do or not to do... Can the "right answer" possibly be a "pass/fail"-criterion regarding your salvation? God has PROMISED that we can KNOW the essential answers.

How should one proceed?

Well, given what we studied about "The Greatest Commandment," will you be more at peace standing in front of God saying, "Lord, not being able to know the hearts of others, I tried to err on the side of agape and support someone in their search for you...", or saying, "Lord, I wanted to be doctrinally precise, and I just didn't believe them when they said they repented, so I turned them away?"

Salvation is available to all, but we must be committed enough to actively pursue it and humble enough to submit to the will of the God who created us and the universe we inhabit.

We must get to know the omniscient, omnipotent, unchanging, ever-loving, merciful, but ultimately just God to whom we must answer.

When we do, the confidence that comes with that knowledge will allow us to approach the end of our walk on this earth humbly and gratefully with a calm mind and a joyous anticipation of what comes next.

Bow before His will and know peace.

APPENDIX 1:
THE PRODIGAL'S PATH

Those who have known a life of faithful service to God and then drifted away are burdened with guilt and shame for having shamefully treated the precious gift of salvation and grace that God has given us all. That shame can make them hesitate to take the first steps back in the right direction because they might have forgotten the story of the Prodigal Son and all the things it teaches us about how God views us and his creation. This book attempts to provide a reminder and encouragement to come home.

Many fall away from their faith because they have set expectations for themselves of levels of perfection that are just not attainable for mortal man. Because while we are supposed to pursue our Christianity with focus and intensity, we will stumble, and we must continue to get up and keep pressing on without stopping to blame ourselves or grinding on how bad our mistake was. The adage "life's a marathon and not a sprint" is so well-worn because it is so true.

In addition to setting the bar too high for themselves, many grow discouraged because of human interpretations of God's will, which have become a tradition and are taught as binding. The advocates for these traditions are typically aggressive and often try to instill guilt in anyone who dares to question or examine the habits or traditions. It is crucial to determine precisely what God has said and to differentiate between that and what decades of human logic and tradition have added.

You can come back

God hasn't given up on you; he wants you back. You are never too far away from God to return. You need to decide to turn around.

Many are discouraged because their impression of God has been formed by people who emphasize God's judgment almost to the point of ignoring God's love and grace for us. This perspective paints an image of a wrathful, vengeful God just sitting up there on His throne, waiting for us to mess up so that He can throw us into hell. In large part, this type of teaching and preaching is a reaction to the equally flawed attitude at the other end of the spectrum that views God as this benevolent, grandfatherly, Santa Claus-like figure who would never possibly punish his creation for willful disobedience.

The story of the Prodigal Son paints a very different picture of a God who sadly allows us to wander away but joyfully welcomes us back with open arms. It is important to acknowledge both aspects of God's nature: His refusal to interfere with our free will and his loving desire for us to return to him.

> "And he said, "There was a man who had two sons. **12** And the younger of them said to his father, 'Father, give me the share of property that is coming to me.' And he divided his

property between them. **13** Not many days later, the younger son gathered all he had and took a journey into a far country, and there he squandered his property in reckless living. **14** And when he had spent everything, a severe famine arose in that country, and he began to be in need. **15** So he went and hired himself out to one of the citizens of that country, who sent him into his fields to feed pigs. **16** And he was longing to be fed with the pods that the pigs ate, and no one gave him anything.

17 "But when he came to himself, he said, 'How many of my father's hired servants have more than enough bread, but I perish here with hunger! **18** I will arise and go to my father, and I will say to him, "Father, I have sinned against heaven and before you. **19** I am no longer worthy to be called your son. Treat me as one of your hired servants."' **20** And he arose and came to his father. But while he was still a long way off, his father saw him and felt compassion, and ran and embraced him and kissed him. **21** And the son said to him, 'Father, I have sinned against heaven and before you. I am no longer worthy to be called your son.' **22** But the father said to his servants, 'Bring quickly the best robe, and put it on him, and put a ring on his hand, and shoes on his feet. **23** And bring the fattened calf and kill it, and let us eat and celebrate. **24** For this my son was dead, and is alive again; he was lost, and is found.' And they began to celebrate.

25 "Now his older son was in the field, and as he came and drew near to the house, he heard music and dancing. **26** And he called one of the servants and asked what these things meant. **27** And he said to him, 'Your brother has come,

and your father has killed the fattened calf, because he has received him back safe and sound.' **28** *But he was angry and refused to go in. His father came out and entreated him,* **29** *but he answered his father, 'Look, these many years I have served you, and I never disobeyed your command, yet you never gave me a young goat, that I might celebrate with my friends.* **30** *But when this son of yours came, who has devoured your property with prostitutes, you killed the fattened calf for him!'* **31** *And he said to him, 'Son, you are always with me, and all that is mine is yours.* **32** *It was fitting to celebrate and be glad, for this your brother was dead, and is alive; he was lost, and is found.'"*
– Luke 15:11-32

The tale of the "Prodigal Son" is a story of youthful, misguided priorities, gaining wisdom through hardship, that wisdom inspiring needed change, and the unwavering love of a father.

The original working title for this book was "A Prodigal's Roadmap Home," but then I realized that this book isn't the roadmap... the roadmap is the Bible. The book's fundamental message is to look nowhere but to the Bible for authoritative answers. My goal was to convince you to trust God, trust His Word, and "work out your own salvation" by directly digging into God's Word and learning what He wants for us. Once you've advanced to that level of understanding, please pass this book on to someone you think would benefit.

I was raised by a Godly man in a Godly household. As a son, I chafed, rebelled against my father's guidance, and didn't listen nearly enough. Still, I also watched his sacrifices for God, heard the reasoning behind his actions, and experienced the loving forgiveness that true agape inspires. I watched him absorb disappointments, year after year, from those he had considered Christian brethren. And yet, he continued to preach the Gospel faithfully for as long as he thought he could do it effectively. Finally, when he felt like he could no longer be effective as an evangelist, he stopped preaching in a final act of reverence for the Gospel and love for his brethren.

Being the son of someone you respect that much is a good news/bad news situation. The good news is that you have excellent instruction and an example. The bad news is that every mistake and wrong choice you make becomes magnified in your mind by comparison; unchecked, it can weigh on you. If I spend too much time comparing how my father spent most of his life to how I have spent the majority of mine, the feelings of inadequacy can become crushing.

Through my father's love for me, I have a measure of understanding of my heavenly Father's love. I understand that not everyone grows up as blessed as I was in a loving household, and that is yet one more reason for us to look forward to the eternal reward of spending time with the Father who loved us enough to sacrifice his own Son that we might have access to Him and a path to salvation.

One of the other things that I've realized is that there are a lot of well-meaning (I assume) preachers out there who think that they will scold people into heaven. What used to be described as "Fire and Brimstone" preaching is based on a righteous belief that God means what He says in His word. The problem is that these preachers lose track of the fact that each soul's journey to God is voluntary and personal and must be embraced and pursued by each Christian individually. Shrieking at people about damnation and all the ways they can lose their souls doesn't nurture them and help provide them with sustenance for the dark hours when they need the courage to resist temptation. What it does is create doubt about the love of God and the possibility of salvation that Satan uses as a wedge to pry struggling people loose who are clinging to the last vestiges of hope of redemption.

We indeed live in a sinful world with abundant temptations that can lead us astray. God expects us to prioritize our soul's salvation, not covet earthly wealth, seek Godly things, and lay up treasures in heaven. It is also true that God expects us to honor and respect His word, study it, and comply with it. But as we have discussed, the path to salvation, while not easy, **is simple** and **<u>attainable</u>**. Adding hurdles and detours to God's path will have frightening consequences in the final judgment.

All these additions and hypercritical attitudes can break the spirit of young Christians and instill a sense of inadequacy and hopelessness, manifested in the attitude of, "Well if it's impossible for me to live up to all these (non-Biblical) standards and I'm going to hell anyway, why not just do all the things that my worldly friends are doing?" So, they wander away and can often create real messes in their lives that must be untangled.

So, whether it is purely a seduction by the world's temptations, hopelessness born of a twisted view of God's will, or some other set of factors, many souls find themselves in a spiritual "far country" yearning to be right with God again.

The story of the Prodigal Son is especially comforting to me in this context. I remember my dad teaching a lesson on the passage and pointing out that the father saw the son returning "while he was yet afar off." He made the point that it wasn't hard to imagine that the father constantly scanned the horizon, hoping to see his son return.

Sadly, my spiritual life has resembled the story of the Prodigal Son. A good upbringing gave way to a period of wandering and mistakes as I strayed. I clung to the memory of what I knew to be right, and over time, I slowly corrected my course and my emphasis on finding out what God wanted me to do and be.

As I focused on Biblical Christianity, I realized that many assumptions have become "baked in" to some Christian's view of worship. Over time, some practices have become so routine that questioning them is considered rebellion and heresy. In discussions with those of different Christian-based backgrounds and traditions, when asking questions about the Biblical authority for some practices, I've often been met with bewilderment that I would even ask such questions because they have just seen it done that way for so long that they cannot imagine any other approach.

Among these otherwise fine folks, there seems to be an attitude that the Bible's details don't matter as long as they feel they are good people. In their minds, that will be sufficient to gain entry to an eternal reward.

The problem is that the Bible makes no provisions for drifting into heaven. The Bible clearly states that the Biblical path to salvation is an informed, focused effort to be pleasing to God. The journey is described as a "race," implying earnest, focused effort. As has been discussed previously, God's displeasure toward a casual attitude about Him and his will is made abundantly clear in the Old Testament in the stories of Nadab and Abihu (Leviticus 10:1-7) and Uzzah (1 Chronicles 13:9-10).

From an earthly perspective, these men didn't do anything particularly evil and were not worthy of death. However, God's perspective is the only one that counts in these matters, and we would be well advised to constantly compare our offerings (our manner of life, our worship, etc.) to what God has specified.

So, if you have wandered away from God, either through temptation or just getting caught up in the cares of the world, please give the ideas presented here from God's word some careful consideration and know that if you are breathing, you are never too far to come back, and it isn't "too late."

> *"Brothers, I do not consider that I have made it my own. But one thing I do: forgetting what lies behind and straining forward to what lies ahead,* **14** *I press on toward the goal for the prize of the upward call of God in Christ Jesus."*
> *– Philippians 3:13-14*

APPENDIX 2:
THE LATE WORKER'S HOPE

Satan gets in our heads and uses our shame for our sinful lives as a wedge to try to keep us from drawing near to God, submitting to his will, and finding salvation. If we have never considered God or "been religious," Satan uses that and tells us that we are being "hypocritical" by trying to "cram for finals" as we age. God is telling us otherwise and asserting his dominion with the parable of the laborers in the vineyard.

> *"For the kingdom of heaven is like a master of a house who went out early in the morning to hire laborers for his vineyard.* **2** *After agreeing with the laborers for a denarius a day, he sent them into his vineyard.* **3** *And going out about the third hour he saw others standing idle in the marketplace,* **4** *and to them he said, 'You go into the vineyard too, and whatever is right I will give you.'* **5** *So they went. Going out again about the sixth hour and the ninth hour, he did the same.* **6** *And about the eleventh hour he went out and found others standing. And*

he said to them, 'Why do you stand here idle all day?' **7** *They said to him, 'Because no one has hired us.' He said to them, 'You go into the vineyard too.'* **8** *And when evening came, the owner of the vineyard said to his foreman, 'Call the laborers and pay them their wages, beginning with the last, up to the first.'* **9** *And when those hired about the eleventh hour came, each of them received a denarius.* **10** *Now when those hired first came, they thought they would receive more, but each of them also received a denarius.* **11** *And on receiving it they grumbled at the master of the house,* **12** *saying, 'These last worked only one hour, and you have made them equal to us who have borne the burden of the day and the scorching heat.'* **13** *But he replied to one of them, 'Friend, I am doing you no wrong. Did you not agree with me for a denarius?* **14** *Take what belongs to you and go. I choose to give to this last worker as I give to you.* **15** *Am I not allowed to do what I choose with what belongs to me? Or do you begrudge my generosity?'* **16** *So the last will be first, and the first last."*
— *Matthew 20:1-16*

God knows what he desires, and we must believe his word is true. This parable promises that no matter how late we may turn to Him, we can have confidence in receiving the reward. There is no "too late" to start.

From our limited earthly perspective, it is understandable to sympathize with the early workers who worked the entire day only to see the same reward given to those who had just shown up—earthly concepts of "fairness" rebel at that apparent inequity. But God clearly communicates who is in charge and limits where a man can presume to judge.

The early workers agreed to a wage and were, therefore, fairly paid. The fact that the lord of the vineyard chose to pay the late workers the same wage was his and only his business.

> *"For my thoughts are not your thoughts,*
> *neither are your ways my ways, declares the Lord.*
> **9** *For as the heavens are higher than the earth,*
> *so are my ways higher than your ways*
> *and my thoughts than your thoughts."*
> *– Isaiah 55:8-9*

The lord of the vineyard going into the town that last time is also in line with the way that Jesus went and sought out sinners and engaged them, giving them the opportunity to turn (e.g., the Samaritan woman John 4:1-31, the calling of Matthew Matt 9:9-12, etc.). God wants you to come back.

As noted earlier, God loved His creation so much that he was willing to sacrifice his son to atone for humanity's sinfulness.

> *"For God so loved the world, that he gave his only Son, that whoever believes in him should not perish but have eternal life."*
> *– John 3:16*

Many are given diagnoses of fatal illnesses weeks or months in advance. I wonder how many hesitate to turn to God because of a feeling of hypocrisy. As mortals, we struggle to understand God's love and how He could forgive a lifetime of rebellion when we only turn and reach for Him at the last moment. This parable of the late workers emphasizes that God is not watching the clock. He is watching our hearts and whether we are willing to submit to His will.

Don't delay

However, the moment you become convicted of your sins and repent and want to turn to God, you should act immediately. Don't assume you have time to think about it further. You must confess God before men and be baptized to wash away your sins.

Notice that the Ethiopian eunuch didn't delay when he believed. He acted immediately.

> *"And the eunuch said to Philip, "About whom, I ask you, does the prophet say this, about himself or about someone else?" **35** Then Philip opened his mouth, and beginning with this Scripture he told him the good news about Jesus. **36** And as they were going along the road they came to some water, and the eunuch said, "See, here is water! What prevents me from being baptized?" **37** And Philip said, "If you believe with all your heart, you may." And he replied, 'I believe that Jesus Christ is the Son of God.' **38** And he commanded the chariot to stop, and they both went down into the water, Philip and the eunuch, and he baptized him. **39** And when they came up out of the water, the Spirit of the Lord carried Philip away, and the eunuch saw him no more, and went on his way rejoicing."*
> – Acts 8:34-39 (Inclusion of v.37 mine)

There is a story that is part of Farish family lore about a family member who decided one night while out camping that he wanted to be baptized. It was late and chilly, and they were sitting around a nice warm campfire, but he had made the decision, and true to the example of the Ethiopian eunuch, it needed to be handled immediately. So, he and his father trudged down to the nearby smelly stock pond, and he was baptized in the middle of the night by flashlight.

Don't put it off. When you know you need to do it, someone will help.

No one deserves salvation

One of the faulty premises that gets into people's heads and prevents them from turning to Jesus is the idea that they don't "deserve" to be saved.

No conscious, responsible adult in the world today deserves to be saved. Not one. Not the most regular pew-warmer, not the most eloquent preacher, not the most devout philanthropist. No one. We ALL have a hope of salvation solely because of the grace of God and the sacrifice of His son, Jesus. Anyone desiring salvation has only to reach for it.

God has carefully described what "reaching for it" looks like and has PROMISED that if we ask, it will be given; if we seek, we shall find; and if we knock, it shall be opened unto us. There are so many powerful passages in the New Testament, but this one booms like a foghorn in a misty harbor to the struggling Christian, signaling "salvation is this way."

Remember the "Ask, Seek, Knock Promise."

How do I join the church?

If you've never been affiliated with any religious organization or want to ensure that you are worshipping God the "right way," you might be asking, "Great! How do I join up?"

> ***Warning** This portion of the book contains a lot of my own thoughts on the church and my conjecture about perceptions of salvation versus realities of salvation. While the thoughts here are intended to represent my honest efforts and are based on what I've read in the Bible, the WHOLE POINT of this book is that you must read the Bible for yourself and draw your own conclusions.*

This is where traditions and the English language can cause some confusion. The word "church" in our modern usage is ambiguous and represents three very different collections of people, as we'll see.

Becoming a part of God's church is unlike joining the Army, the football team, a country club, or some other earthly organization.

In the following figure, I've tried to graphically represent the three main ways the word "church" is commonly used today.

The concepts/ideas I'm trying to illustrate here are:

1) You may "join" a "**Named Church** [2]" or a "**Local church (Congregation)** [3]", but God must add you to "**God's church** [1]."

2) The distinctions lie in who is controlling the population.

Many folks fail to distinguish the church from earthly organizations (clubs, fraternities, etc.), so they try to apply the same processes to becoming a part of the church. Their confusion is partly because of the ambiguity of the modern word "church." The only church that matters is the church which is the collection of all who have surrendered their will and obedience to the all-powerful creator of the universe. When that happens, God Almighty is the one who adds that soul to the church (represented in the diagram below as "**God's church** [1]").

Groups of Christians who live near each other gathering to worship are referred to as "churches" in the New Testament (e.g., 1 Corinthians 1:3, Galatians 1:1, etc.) represented in the diagram below as "**Local church (congregation)** [3]", but care should be given never to confuse being a part of those local groups and being part of the true church. There are also examples in the New Testament of people (apparently) being part of one of these local groups but behaving in such a way as to call into question whether they were a part of the true church. (e.g., Diotrophes, 3 John 1:9)

However, to further confuse things, over the years, humanity has added a third organizational structure and chose to refer to it as "church," and that is the broader collection of local congregations who have all agreed on a shared understanding and application of scripture, often adding an extra-Biblical organization and management structure. These are often referred to as "denominations," but for purposes of this discussion, I've chosen to represent them in the diagram below as "Named Churches (2)." You can think of them as groups of "Local churches (congregation) (3)" who claim a shared set of beliefs.

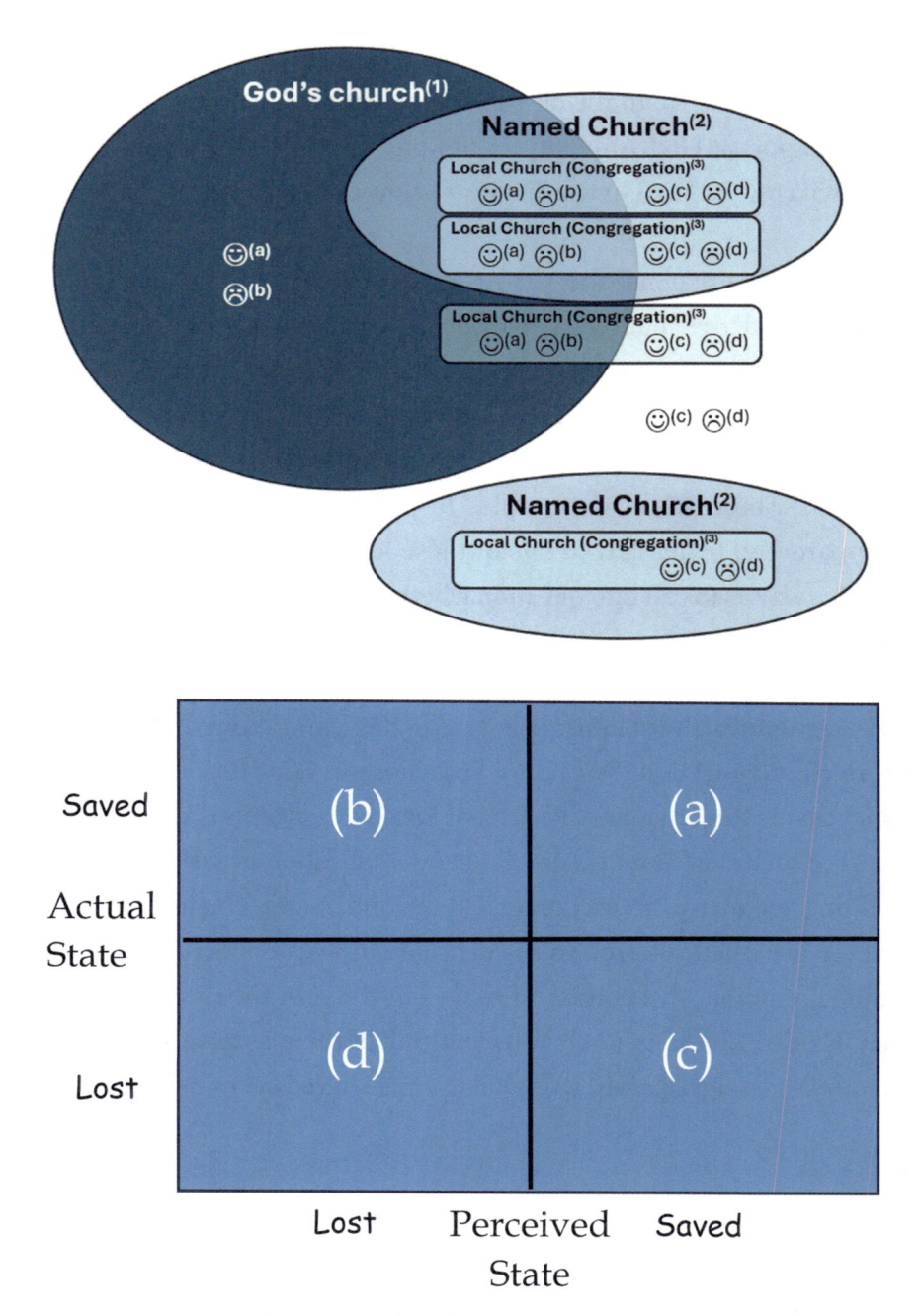

Figure 1 - Lost/Saved Perception Matrix

The little smiley and frowny emoticons only indicate the person's *perception* of their state of salvation. They might think they are spiritually in a good place (as represented by (c)), but only God determines whether we are acceptable to Him.

The goal of this book is obviously to help people not only get into the "(a)" and "(b)" boxes on the salvation matrix but also to help them get to "(a)," where they can live a life of contentment and face their eventual reunion with God with confidence and joy.

"(c)" People will be challenging to reach because without an awareness of need, why change?

That leaves "(d)" folks ("lost and know it"), and I hope that this book can help these folks know that there is a path to God and that he is waiting and hoping for their turn to Him.

Please forgive me for straying into the world of Venn diagrams and quadrant charts, but they help me sort things out in my head, and if they provoke you to think and discuss, I'll consider that a "win."

How does the Bible describe becoming a part of "the church"?

> *"Now when they **heard** this they **were cut to the heart**, and said to Peter and the rest of the apostles, "Brothers, what shall we do?"* **38** *And Peter said to them, "**Repent** and **be baptized** every one of **you in the name of Jesus Christ for the forgiveness of your sins**, and you will receive the gift of the Holy Spirit.* **39** *For the promise is for you and for your children and for all who are far off, everyone whom the Lord our God calls to himself."* **40** *And with many other*

words he bore witness and continued to exhort them, saying, "Save yourselves from this crooked generation." **41** *So those who received his word were baptized, and there were added that day about three thousand souls."*
– Acts 2:37-41 (emphasis mine)

How do I come to God?

The story of Philip and the Ethiopian Eunuch (Acts 8:34-39) we examined earlier gives about as brief a description of the process of coming to God, which can be found in the scriptures.

The **first step** in coming to God is to **hear** the gospel or the "good news" of salvation. (Acts 8:35)

The **second step** in coming to God is to **believe** that gospel. (Acts 8:37)

It is important to note that simple belief was not enough. The Ethiopian eunuch still had to act on his belief to be saved.

The **third step**, specified in Acts 2:38, is to **repent** from our Godless life and to turn to God.

The **fourth step** is to **confess** that belief. (Acts 8:37)

The **fifth step** is to be **baptized**. (Acts 8:38)

The step that doesn't get explicitly called out in the story of the Ethiopian Eunuch is **repentance**, the "thinking differently afterward" or "changed after being with" that the believer feels when they accept the Gospel. But the account in Acts 2:37-38 spells out the place of repentance in the path to salvation.

And Mark tells us of Jesus describing the act of repentance as part of believing in the gospel.

> *"Now after John was arrested, Jesus came into Galilee, proclaiming the gospel of God,* **15** *and saying, 'The time is fulfilled, and the kingdom of God is at hand;* **repent** *and believe in the gospel.'"*
> *– Mark 1:14-15 (emphasis mine)*

So... there are five steps:

1) **Hear** the gospel
2) **Believe** in the gospel
3) **Repent** of your sins
4) **Confess** Jesus as the Son of God
5) **Be Baptized** for the remission of your sins

...and at the end of those steps, we are told that God adds anyone who sincerely walks this path to the church.

> *"...And* **the Lord added** *to their number day by day those who were being saved."*
> *– Acts 2:47 (emphasis mine)*

Unfortunately, many people think that everything after that is autopilot when they get to this point in the process, and they don't have anything else to do. I shiver a little every time I hear someone say, "I got saved..." because the implication is that their salvation was a one-step action and not an ongoing process of submission to God's will. A careful consideration of scripture will reveal a different truth.

> *"You therefore, beloved, knowing this beforehand, take care that you are not carried away with the error of lawless people and lose your own stability."*
> *– 2 Peter 3:17*

> *"Now the Spirit expressly says that in later times some will depart from the faith by devoting themselves to deceitful spirits and teachings of demons, **2** through the insincerity of liars whose consciences are seared, **3** who forbid marriage and require abstinence from foods that God created to be received with thanksgiving by those who believe and know the truth."*
> *– 1 Timothy 4:1-3*

Baptism represents a "re-birth," as with any other birth; there is a life to be lived and things to be done. Many of these points have been addressed elsewhere already, but here is a quick reference, which is by no means exhaustive.

- Study
    - *"Do your best to present yourself to God as one approved, a worker who has no need to be ashamed, rightly handling the word of truth."*
        - *2 Timothy 2:15*
- Grow
    - *"But grow in the grace and knowledge of our Lord and Savior Jesus Christ. To him be the glory both now and to the day of eternity. Amen."*
        - *2 Peter 3:18*

- Worship
  - *"But the hour is coming, and is now here, when the true worshipers will worship the Father in spirit and truth, for the Father is seeking such people to worship him."*
    – John 4:23
- Serve
  - *"Religion that is pure and undefiled before God the Father is this: to visit orphans and widows in their affliction, and to keep oneself unstained from the world."*
    – James 1:27
- Forgive
  - *"For if you forgive others their trespasses, your heavenly Father will also forgive you,* **15** *but if you do not forgive others their trespasses, neither will your Father forgive your trespasses."*
    – Matthew 6:14-15
  - *"Judge not, and you will not be judged; condemn not, and you will not be condemned; forgive, and you will be forgiven;"*
    – Luke 6:37
  - *"Then Peter came up and said to him, "Lord, how often will my brother sin against me, and I forgive him? As many as seven times?"* **22** *Jesus said to him, "I do not say to you seven times, but seventy-seven times."*
    – Matthew 18:21-22
- Share the Gospel
  - *"And he said to them, "Go into all the world and proclaim the gospel to the whole creation.*
    16 *Whoever believes and is baptized will be saved, but whoever does not believe will be condemned."*
    – Mark 16: 15-16

- Pray constantly!
  - *"Rejoice always, **17** pray without ceasing, **18** give thanks in all circumstances; for this is the will of God in Christ Jesus for you."*

    — 1 Thessalonians 5:16-18
- Do all of it with Agape (love)
  - *"If I speak in the tongues of men and of angels, but have not love, I am a noisy gong or a clanging cymbal. **2** And if I have prophetic powers, and understand all mysteries and all knowledge, and if I have all faith, so as to remove mountains, but have not love, I am nothing. **3** If I give away all I have, and if I deliver up my body to be burned, but have not love, I gain nothing. 4 Love is patient and kind; love does not envy or boast; it is not arrogant **5** or rude. It does not insist on its own way; it is not irritable or resentful; **6** it does not rejoice at wrongdoing, but rejoices with the truth. **7** Love bears all things, believes all things, hopes all things, endures all things. **8** Love never ends. As for prophecies, they will pass away; as for tongues, they will cease; as for knowledge, it will pass away. **9** For we know in part and we prophesy in part, **10** but when the perfect comes, the partial will pass away. **11** When I was a child, I spoke like a child, I thought like a child, I reasoned like a child. When I became a man, I gave up childish ways. **12** For now we see in a mirror dimly, but then face to face. Now I know in part; then I shall know fully, even as I have been fully known. **13** So now faith, hope, and love abide, these three; but the greatest of these is love."*

    — 1 Corinthians 13

With whom do I worship?

A part of our path to salvation is helping others along the way. One way that we do that is by gathering to worship God as a "Local church (congregation)" mentioned earlier. The New Testament describes and patterns this, and while a detailed examination of that is outside the scope of this discussion, there are a few key points to consider.

First and foremost, the group must genuinely desire to prioritize God's will over any other consideration. That requires study and prayer. You are not looking for a social club; you are looking for a group of those in God's church who you can help and who can help you find your way to God.

It does not have to be a large group.

> *"For where two or three are gathered in my name, there am I among them."*
> *– Matthew 18:20*

Selectiveness about the people with whom you worship is a Biblical principle. We gather to worship God and to give and receive encouragement, not to dump our stress and frustrations from the week on someone else or to have someone else take their bad week out on us.

> *"I appeal to you, brothers, to watch out for those who cause divisions and create obstacles contrary to the doctrine that you have been taught; avoid them. 18 For such persons do not serve our Lord Christ, but their own appetites, and by smooth talk and flattery, they deceive the hearts of the naive."*
> *– Romans 16:17-18*

Several passages seem to get overlooked or neglected for some reason, but in my experience, this passage ranks very close to the top of the list. How often have you seen someone gossip, maneuver, and criticize without being corrected or admonished?

While I cannot know anyone else's heart, I can observe their actions and listen to the words that come out of their mouths. If those do not align with my understanding of God's word, I have a responsibility to go to them in love and concern. But that tender, caring approach is a very different one from a holier-than-thou chastisement for their weakness, and sadly, there are some who cannot see the distinction.

> "***You will recognize them by their fruits***. *Are grapes gathered from thornbushes, or figs from thistles?* **17** *So, every healthy tree bears good fruit, but the diseased tree bears bad fruit.* **18** *A healthy tree cannot bear bad fruit, nor can a diseased tree bear good fruit.* **19** *Every tree that does not bear good fruit is cut down and thrown into the fire.* **20** *Thus **you will recognize them by their fruits**.*"
> – Matthew 7:16-20 (emphasis mine)

You are seeking to worship with a group of Christians who are serious about examining God's word and conforming themselves to it, not figuring out excuses to justify what they want to do, how they want to live or how they prefer to offer worship to the Lord.

You are not looking for a place to be entertained, a place to make social connections, or to expand your business network.

As in everything, make your decision with prayer, asking, seeking, and knocking.

Made in the USA
Columbia, SC
14 September 2024